BAZAAR
STYLE

photography by Debi Treloar

BAZAAR STYLE

Decorating with market and vintage finds

Selina Lake

with words by Joanna Simmons

RYLAND
PETERS
& SMALL

LONDON NEW YORK

Senior Designer Amy Trombat
Senior Editor Clare Double
Location Research Selina Lake, Jess Walton
Production Gemma John
Publishing Director Alison Starling
Art Director Leslie Harrington

Styling Selina Lake

First published in the US in 2008
by Ryland Peters & Small
519 Broadway, 5th Floor
New York, NY 10012
www.rylandpeters.com

Text copyright © Joanna Simmons 2008
Design and photographs copyright
© Ryland Peters & Small 2008

10 9 8 7 6 5 4 3 2 1

Printed and bound in China.

Library of Congress Cataloging-in-Publication
Data

Lake, Selina.
  Bazaar style : decorating with market and
vintage finds / Selina Lake ; photography by
Debi Treloar ; with words by Joanna Simmons.
-- 1st U.S. ed.
    p. cm.
  Includes index.
  ISBN 978-1-84597-626-2
  1. Found objects (Art) in interior decoration.
  2. Antiques in interior decoration. I. Title.
  NK2115.5.F68L35 2008
  747--dc22
                      2007038244

CONTENTS

INTRODUCTION

From a Turkish market with hundreds of booths groaning under the weight of fabrics, spices, and trinkets to a village fair selling everything from homemade jam to secondhand books, bazaars the world over are all about abundance. There's plenty to see and much to delight the senses. Bazaar style encapsulates all this color, richness, and diversity—and brings it home. The look is relaxed and individual, with rooms that are comfortable, maybe a little quirky, but always full of interest.

Bazaar style is the antidote to interiors magazines listing must-have products and the latest colors. It doesn't follow fashion or obey rules, but allows you to set your imagination free, mixing furniture and fabrics from across the decades. It's a look that is easy to pull off because anything goes, from vintage and retro to recycled and restored. There's no snobbery in a bazaar-style home. Pieces inherited from a great-aunt can be cherished alongside something found on a foreign vacation. No item is off-limits, either. Shabby objects can be quickly refreshed—a lick of white eggshell paint can transform a tired dresser, or a row of sequins rev up a plain pillow.

Flea markets, estate sales, antique shops, and eBay are rich hunting grounds, all offering an element of surprise—you never know what you're going to find. From foreign treasures such as French linen tablecloths to English country classics like floral tea sets and rustic baskets. From retro wallpapers to Scottish woolen blankets, oil paintings to old mirrors. Pieces that have lived long or traveled far come with personality built in. A lantern that you haggled for in a foreign market; a neglected chair you found in a French *brocante* fair; a frayed throw you nursed back to life with needle and thread; these items will give your home life and soul. How much nicer to have a rug made

9

using traditional artisan techniques than a factory-produced alternative? How much more interesting to have furniture that tells a story than a mass-produced flat-pack piece, cheap to buy, but hard to value?

The bazaar look cannot be bought on one shopping trip. It grows organically over the years, with finds gathered from diverse sources. It celebrates the beauty of our everyday possessions, too—almost anything can look striking when thoughtfully arranged and given room to breathe—and loves color. Think of the rich tones of Moroccan kilims on a souk stall, the flowers in a European market, or the colors on the spines of old paperbacks in a secondhand bookstore. Color used bravely and abundantly can inspire, refresh, and invigorate the senses. Most of us feel better with some color in our lives.

Bazaar Style will show you where to shop, what to look for, and how to put it all together. There is a wealth of inspiration to be found in the interiors shown on these pages, and by seeing what others have done in their homes you'll gain confidence to experiment in yours. Perhaps you have never dared to hang a floral painting, picked up in a thrift shop, against flowery wallpaper or had not guessed that granny's old pitcher could look so good as a vase. You might not have thought of showing off your jewelry in a beautiful old teacup, or keeping kitchen dishes in an old armoire. By absorbing the unusual combinations and innovative ways in which everyday objects have been made to look exceptional, you'll begin to master a whole new style. Happily, it's one that need not cost much and isn't hard to achieve. Just have fun and follow your instincts.

elements

FURNITURE *and* STORAGE

From an antique chaise longue recovered in lush velvet to a swiveling Sixties chair found in a flea market, furniture that shouts individuality is key to the bazaar look. The odd modern classic or simple piece bought in the mall may find its way into a bazaar-style home, but generally its rooms are stuffed with furniture that has seen a bit of life and has the personality to prove it.

ABOVE LEFT *A humble chest of drawers offers invaluable storage and looks good in almost any room. Paint a tired pine piece white to refresh it, then create a display of collectibles on top. A feathered wall decoration, hanging above, provides a shot of glamour, too.*

BELOW LEFT *Shoes are objects of beauty in their own right, so enjoy their colors and design when you're not wearing them by arranging them on open shelves.*

OPPOSITE *Books add life to any room, but don't need to be neatly lined up on conventional shelves, library-style. Here, a clear plexiglass unit is home to a collection of oversized hardbacks.*

The joy of buying secondhand is that you have so much choice. A modern furniture store will sell beds, sofas, armchairs, tables—formulaic pieces designed for a single purpose. Go shopping for old furniture, however, think laterally, and a world of options opens up. First, there's the exciting surprise element —you cannot predict what will take your fancy, from a French wrought-iron daybed to a slim Seventies sideboard. Then, if you consider how objects meant for one function can be adapted to another, further opportunities present themselves. A hospital trolley can work as a side table; a department store display cabinet can be a cavernous chest of drawers; an old tea chest makes a good TV stand.

Secondhand pieces are, by definition, old and well used, but that doesn't mean their quality has been compromised.

They were often made using skills and materials rarely found in today's mass-produced furniture industry. You may have to give them a makeover, but you're getting a piece made with care and expertise, already proven to have stood the test of time, and often at a bargain price. Buying secondhand is ethical, too, sitting comfortably with today's emphasis on recycling and reusing. With so much enticing, good-quality furniture out there already, why buy new?

Thrift shops, house clearance sales, and flea markets are good sources of interesting secondhand furniture. Internet auction sites such as eBay also offer rich pickings, but check the measurements of any item carefully before you bid. It is easy to get carried away, only to bid successfully on a piece that will not fit anywhere in your home or looks disappointingly small when

THIS PAGE *We often rely on collectibles and art to add color and decoration to a room, but a show-stopping armchair brings drama that you can curl up in. The owner found it in a dumpster and had it painted and upholstered in crimson.*

OPPOSITE LEFT *This La Chaise chair by Charles and Ray Eames is a modern classic. Its white fiberglass shell and modernist design look even more striking set against a contrasting bazaar-style backdrop of patterned wallpaper.*

OPPOSITE RIGHT *Sensual velvet makes a wonderful upholstery fabric, and these cute armchairs, covered in brilliant pink, feel as good as they look. Different floral patterns have been layered on in this living space, but a color theme of rich pink unites the scheme.*

RIGHT *An elegant French armchair, found in a thrift shop, is given a feminine makeover with pink paint on its frame and patterned silk upholstery.*

OPPOSITE, ABOVE LEFT *This ornate armchair has been reborn in striking style with a metallic painted frame and black upholstery.*

OPPOSITE, ABOVE RIGHT *Retro orange leather chairs with tubular frames are softened with patterned and animal-hide cushions.*

OPPOSITE, BELOW LEFT *This sofa is covered with a fabric by Marimekko. Printed with branches and leaves, rather than a repeat pattern, it makes the sofa look like a piece of art.*

OPPOSITE, BELOW RIGHT *A green leather and metal armchair is an eye-catching addition to this living space. A backdrop of glossy black painted floorboards and white walls is all it needs to look its best.*

it arrives. Weigh up delivery and transportation costs, too—you may be able to afford something more expensive if it's local.

The bazaar look is not necessarily about buying everything cheaply, however. You may want to blow the budget on a fabulous designer chair, but find the rest of your living-room furniture in flea markets. A contemporary item or design classic will look doubly arresting alongside painted furniture and squashy sofas than in the more predictable setting of a modernist room. It is the combination of objects that makes a bazaar-style scheme exciting, so buy something because you love it, not because it matches what you already own. Passion for the piece is all that matters.

When hunting for big pieces of furniture like sofas and chairs, you will be drawn to their style first, but you should also look at how they are made. A solid wooden frame and a well-sprung, comfortable seat with stuffing intact are important—putting these right is expensive. Reupholstering, on the other hand, is easier to do and, while reasonably costly (expect to pay a few hundred dollars for a small armchair), it allows you to choose the fabric. A cheap alternative is to layer a worn sofa, chaise, or chair with throws, old linen sheets, or tactile lambskins to refresh its appearance, or have simple slipcovers made. When it comes to beds, think about combining old and new for a happy marriage of style and comfort. An old wooden or iron frame looks great, and when teamed with a new mattress you get a bed that feels wonderful, too.

Remember to look beyond appearances to see each item's full potential. That way, you will have the pick of the pieces that

ABOVE LEFT *This filing cabinet was once gray, but has been reinvented with floral paper, stuck to its drawers. It makes a lively contrast to the simple wooden shelving.*

ABOVE RIGHT *Displaying ordinary things and enjoying their beauty is an idea at the heart of bazaar style, and in this kitchen a simple glass-fronted unit allows its brightly colored inhabitants to be appreciated.*

others overlook. Wonky hinges and missing knobs can be replaced on armoires, chests, and cabinets. Varnish can be stripped and some nourishing wax used in its place for a fresh look. The most dreary armchair can look outstanding when newly covered with a retro fabric or plush velour, and bright paint can do much to disguise the unexciting shape of a wooden bookshelf or chest of drawers.

When it comes to storage, built-in units and cabinets can make the most of an awkward corner or create storage in an unlikely location (above a door, say, or under the stairs), but they can be expensive to have specially made and, of course, cannot travel with you when you move. You may prefer to opt for freestanding pieces instead, or a mixture of both. In a kitchen,

an old armoire makes a roomy home for china, while wall-hung units can store food. In the bedroom, open shelves can hold shoes and handbags, and a closet house clothes.

Remember, too, that bazaar-style homes celebrate the beauty in everyday objects, so don't hide all your possessions behind sleek cupboard doors: have most of them on show, but organized; visible, but ordered. To do this, look for versatile storage such as baskets, glass-fronted cabinets, shelves, wooden fruit or wine crates, retail display units, trolleys, and hooks. Use them to store everything from towels to teacups, clothes to china.

For those possessions that do need to be stored out of sight, there are plenty of pieces that provide practicality with personality. An old map chest or wooden filing cabinet can hold

ABOVE LEFT *Wooden hutches are chunky classics, teaming practical storage with open shelves for display. The painting by Jenny Jones depicts the house owners on their wedding day.*

ABOVE RIGHT *Teaming an oversized gooseneck lamp with traditional pieces—a chandelier and pretty china—gives this dining space a sense of humor. Playing with scale and mixing styles is central to bazaar style.*

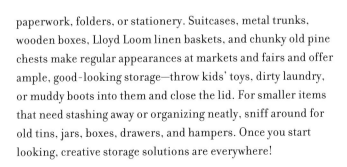

paperwork, folders, or stationery. Suitcases, metal trunks, wooden boxes, Lloyd Loom linen baskets, and chunky old pine chests make regular appearances at markets and fairs and offer ample, good-looking storage—throw kids' toys, dirty laundry, or muddy boots into them and close the lid. For smaller items that need stashing away or organizing neatly, sniff around for old tins, jars, boxes, drawers, and hampers. Once you start looking, creative storage solutions are everywhere!

ABOVE LEFT *Shoes and handbags arranged on open shelves look like an art installation and give a room lots of personality.*

ABOVE RIGHT *Bazaar style is not about keeping your possessions behind closed doors. Here, a simple unit is home to colorful baskets and shoes, bringing visual interest, color, and texture to the room.*

OPPOSITE *The patterned textiles and reclaimed furniture give this teenager's bedroom a laidback, pretty look. The blackboard paint on the walls allows her to chalk up her own art. The lampshade is made from old buttons and the curtains from terrycloth. A found retail display cabinet is now used as a chest of drawers.*

ABOVE *A floral theme links the faded fabric of this sofa with the vibrant pillows. The embroidered sunflowers introduce lashings of texture.*

RIGHT *A mismatched combination of sheets, quilts, and pillowcases gives this bed a relaxed, pretty look. By layering the bedding, no single pattern is allowed to dominate, but all have a chance to shine.*

OPPOSITE *Two different patterns coexist happily here. The wallpaper is traditional, while the pillow, made from vintage fabric remnants, is unmistakably Seventies. By sitting the pillow on a chair of similar color, the eye is drawn to them, while the wallpaper melts into the background.*

TEXTILES

Curtains, upholstery, throws, bedding, cushions—textiles crop up in every room of the house and can bring it beautifully to life. They marry texture, pattern, and color, three essential ingredients of bazaar style, and can take an interior from ordinary to individual in an instant. The trick is to team a variety of textiles together to create a rich visual and sensual mix.

Introducing textiles into any scheme is quick and inexpensive. In a living room, mix and match scatter cushions, bringing in new ones and rotating old as you fancy. Use fabric remnants to make a relaxed throw or customize a simple readymade pillow by stitching on sequins, tassels, or felt flowers. In a bedroom, ditch the matching bedlinen in favor of a melange of pretty patterns on comforters, bedspreads, and pillowcases, picked up at markets or secondhand stores. Hang delicate vintage lace at a window to diffuse the light and add rich damask curtains for privacy at night. Wake up an old coffee table or bedside cabinet

by covering it with a length of fabric, then top it off with a pane of glass cut to fit. In your work space, use an old linen tablecloth or a thick Indian bedspread to cover a tired desk. If your workstation is in an open-plan living area, create some privacy by sectioning it off with pretty voile, glass curtains, or vintage silk scarves pinned together.

The world is your shopping oyster when you're looking for textiles that suit the bazaar look. Ethnic outlets are excellent hunting grounds for jewel-bright sari fabric, swatches of shimmering Thai silk, or Moroccan rugs and bedspreads in spicy

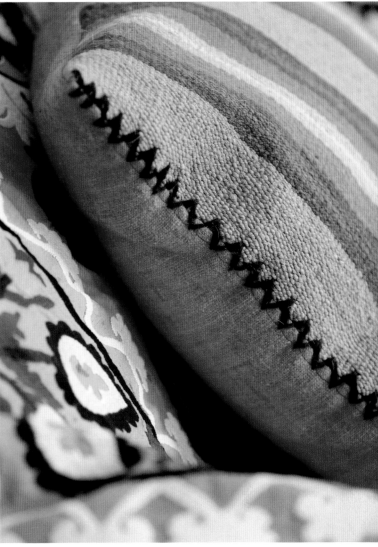

colors. Flea markets will generally have a selection of old rugs that, when professionally cleaned, can look superb, alongside plenty of fabric remnants of all types of material, old curtains, and clothes. Try eBay for original fabrics from every decade of the 20th century, and don't rule out reproductions, either—many shops (including the chains) sell scatter cushions and lampshades in prints inspired by Seventies psychedelia or vintage florals that look just as good as the real thing.

When you're working textiles into your home, remember to think outside the decorating box. Sari fabric can make a pretty canopy for a bed. Sarongs and shawls make excellent throws for sofas or armchairs, as do old blankets and patchwork quilts.

ABOVE LEFT *By picking a floral theme, pillows in a range of different vintage fabrics from across the decades can look wonderful together.*

ABOVE RIGHT *Ethnic textiles are often made with strong, bright, saturated colors. Here, a Moroccan cushion sits against an embroidered Indian throw, their shared palette making them a great team.*

OPPOSITE *Pale walls and plenty of pink and red give this living space energy. Moroccan pillows bring a simple sofa to life, their color echoed in the paintings above. Artist Ana Drummond made the "Just Say No Thank You" painting.*

THIS PAGE *This comfortable old sofa in a gazebo is layered with blankets, throws, and cushions to give it bright and inviting color and texture. Piling on the textiles has the added benefit of concealing worn seats or frayed upholstery.*

OPPOSITE LEFT *Square floor cushions covered in fantastically bright textiles are a flexible, informal alternative to a traditional sofa. Supplement them with matching cushions that can be propped against the wall to boost comfort and a cozy blanket for relaxed, low-level lounging.*

OPPOSITE RIGHT *A pile of fabric swatches in brilliant colors forms a striking display. Keep them on open shelves or piled in a basket until you are ready to fashion them into pillow covers or throws —or just enjoy them as they are.*

Secondhand curtains can be cut up to make pillow covers, as can old wool sweaters or vintage dresses and shirts—all you need is a sewing machine and a spare afternoon. A curtain may not offer enough material to make a tablecloth, but it could be reborn as pretty placemats. If you love the pattern of a fabric remnant, frame it for some instant artwork.

The bazaar look often incorporates textiles into a room just for the sheer joy of having them there—they need not serve a practical purpose. So if you find a delicious swatch of old fabric

or a lovely old curtain, hang it against a wall as a tactile artwork or across a doorway as a partition. Tack lengths of lace or strips of patterned fabric above a window or along a tabletop edge. Pin a collection of handkerchiefs or napkins to a wall or door. Pile up fabric remnants, waiting to be fashioned into pillowcases or cushion covers, in an old basket or on a shelf so you can enjoy their color and pattern before you get to work on them.

There are no rules to displaying textiles, only guidelines. Try layering them, so that garish prints don't dominate. Top a wildly

ABOVE LEFT *Fabrics, needlework samplers, and knitted blankets—some family heirlooms —have been arranged on a bench, simply to be enjoyed in all their variety.*

ABOVE RIGHT *Old lace and delicately woven fabrics crop up at markets and fairs regularly and make great window treatments. This lace panel helps provide privacy, while the heavy embroidered fabric that covers the console table below makes a tactile contrast.*

OPPOSITE *An eclectic mix of patterns, textures, and textiles lives in this bedroom, from the exotic wallpaper to the floral fabric canopy. The bedspread was made from lengths of traditional Dutch ribbon, painstakingly stitched together.*

printed bed sheet with a faded quilt to tame it, for example—you still get to enjoy the lively pattern, but it won't walk all over your bedroom. Don't be afraid to clash textiles, either, but reduce the visual shock by finding one unifying element—a key color or a similar pattern, be that floral, geometric, or retro.

Remember to mix in plenty of texture, too. A room that invites you to reach out and touch it is more relaxing and welcoming than one that simply looks great. The tactile surprise of finding a silk scatter cushion next to a mohair one, a fake-fur throw next to a cotton one, is pleasing and exciting. Enjoy exploring the range of textures that just one material can offer, too. Wool, for example, can be thick and reassuring in an old Welsh blanket, or incredibly soft and sensual in the form of merino wool from Spain, famous for its extra-long fibers.

THIS PAGE *Colors are bold, blocky, and brilliant in this living space. There is very little pattern in the scheme here, but a great deal of strong, bright color. Neutral walls and glossy black floorboards create a simple backdrop for the huge artwork, graphic cushions, and striped rug. It's an unfussy, brave look that works well with the clean lines of the designer furniture.*

OPPOSITE *A graphically patterned rug like the one in this living space becomes the eye-catching chief artwork of the room. Walls are left plain and neutral to let it take center stage, while a bright orange sofa and lavender stair carpet continue the colorful theme.*

COLOR
and PATTERN

Throughout history, we have incorporated color, pattern, and decoration into our homes. It is human instinct to decorate and adorn, injecting interest and beauty into our domestic environment. Bazaar style shows you how to use color and pattern beautifully.

ABOVE *China introduces color and pattern on a small scale. Here, pretty plates and a tray share a simple floral design and vibrant colors.*

RIGHT *Vintage Seventies wallpaper bought on eBay creates a bold wall of pattern. A sideboard from a thrift shop looks perfect in front.*

OPPOSITE LEFT *A color theme of gray, black, and white and a mix of geometric shapes and patterns gives this hallway real drama. Seen from this angle, the mirrored unit reflects the rug's pattern, doubling its impact.*

OPPOSITE RIGHT *Colored glass bricks make a beautiful room partition, and their shades are echoed in the chair and rug beyond.*

In medieval times, even simple homes in Europe were often colorfully painted, using limewash mixed with whatever ingredients were on hand—animal blood or yellow ocher. Fabrics were the usual means of adding color to Elizabethan rooms, while in the Georgian period (1760—1830) pastel blues and greens were common on walls, made by mixing copper or iron sulfate into the plaster. In the mid-1800s, when wallpaper production was mechanized and it could be cheaply made, everybody was pasting it up. New dyes were developed, too, so designs in bright colors

hit Victorian homes, jostling for attention alongside heavy curtains, rich rugs, and an abundance of ornaments. Set against this historical context, the recent vogue for paring down, putting away, and using pale colors seems a blip, rather than a lasting trend. We have, it seems, always loved color and pattern.

Paint is an easy and inexpensive way to bring color into your home. Spend an afternoon painting your walls and you can completely reinvent a room for the price of a few gallons. You need not paint every room, or even every wall. To introduce some

LEFT *Liberate pretty, patterned clothes from a closet and hang them up so they make a colorful contribution to a room. Here, the clothes are fitting companions to the brilliant cushions below.*

OPPOSITE, ABOVE LEFT *A papered wall butts up to one that's been roughly painted with a panel of green, creating a casual mish-mash of pattern and color.*

OPPOSITE, ABOVE RIGHT *Perhaps the bare plaster and swatches of wallpaper, taped to the wall, are a decorating job that was never finished—because the owner was distracted by how good this combination looks.*

OPPOSITE, BELOW LEFT *Embroidered handkerchiefs, taped to a wall, make an unusual textural decoration.*

OPPOSITE, BELOW RIGHT *Wallpaper samples create a patchwork effect on this wall.*

color without fear of it dominating, use it as an accent against a neutral backdrop, painting it on a chimney breast or a single wall, or paint the surround of a window to frame the view. Paints suitable for woodwork (gloss, satinwood, and eggshell) are now available in a huge range of shades, too, so bring color to doors, baseboards, and window frames while keeping walls white. Alternatively, paint your floorboards—another effective way to introduce color without splashing it up the walls.

For a combination of pattern and color, look to wallpaper. Enjoying a huge style renaissance today, it is available in a range of designs and prices. You can also find original wallpapers from the 20th century—the internet is a good source. Use it as an accent or artwork, by hanging on one wall, in a chimney alcove, or inside an old picture frame. Creative types can paste scraps

and samples side by side for a patchwork effect. And don't stop there—layer on more pattern by hanging a flower painting or an embroidered dress against floral wallpaper. To find the right paper for you, tack up samples before you buy a whole roll, and, if you're using an expensive wallpaper or one with a complicated pattern, consider paying a professional to hang it.

Fabric and upholstery are two further sources of color and pattern and much used in a bazaar-style room. Scatter vibrant cushions and throws over a neutral sofa and layer crocheted blankets, ethnic bedspreads, and embroidered sheets on a bed. If you are handy with a needle and thread, use a scrap basket of fabric remnants to make pillow covers or slipcovers for sofa and armchair seats—it's a cheap way to revive a battered piece and inject plenty of pattern.

ABOVE *Really bright colors like this lime green can enliven a room and create a talking point. Temper them with neutral walls and simple furniture.*

RIGHT *In this Moroccan house a scattering of cushions with bold flower designs, made from fabric bought locally, create a vibrant fireside seating area.*

OPPOSITE LEFT *Layering color and pattern works well in a bazaar-style room. Here, picture frames pick out the pink, red, and yellow in the wallpaper, while their neat stripes create a graphic contrast. The paper is by Matthew Williamson for Habitat.*

OPPOSITE RIGHT *A simple arrangement of lamp and vases sits well in front of this large-scale wallpaper pattern (Birdtree by Neisha Crosland). A bigger display could look fussy and chaotic.*

When it comes to windows, you'll find mountains of secondhand curtains at flea markets and rummage sales. If the patterns are too wild or faded, customize them with sections of plain cotton, or find an alternative; a tablecloth, sheet, or length of lace might do as well. Floors can get expressive with a colorful, pattern-rich rug. Go ethnic with a spice-toned dhurri from India, retro with a Seventies swirly design, or choose a more organic look with fake zebra-print hides or woven seagrass. Move them from room to room, layer them, or let them peep out from under chairs and tables—rugs are a flexible way to add pattern to your home.

With bazaar style, the more bold and confident you are, the better, but when teaming colors and patterns it's helpful to look for a theme. Choose to lay Moroccan rugs on your floors— you can then pick an array of styles and shades, but their common heritage will pull the look together. Or draw on a shared color— bright yellow and blue Moroccan floor tiles can live happily alongside pillows covered in Sixties fabric of the same color, even though they come from different eras and countries. Look for one uniting factor, be it pattern, color, period, or place of manufacture, to direct your scheme and provide style cohesion.

LIGHTING

We so often overlook lighting when putting together a
room, but it's vitally important. It has the power to
influence the atmosphere, improve our mood, and
help us perform daily tasks, from putting on make-up
to cooking. Lighting plays a key practical role, but that
doesn't mean it must look high-tech. In a bazaar-style
home, built-in fixtures are complemented with quirky
lamps, mismatched shades, and fun fairy lights.

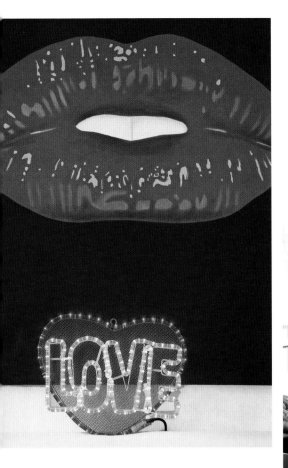

Many modern room schemes place great emphasis on built-in lighting, often featuring rows of recessed spots, track lighting, and even bulbs set into the floor, but the bazaar look favors a more back-to-basics approach, with plenty of table and floor lamps, wall sconces, chandeliers, and decorative shades. This means that, for the majority of your rooms, there's no reason not to light your home as you've furnished it, with a mix of retro, recycled, thrift-shop, and cheap-chic pieces picked up over the years, at home and abroad.

Before we get excited about the bazaar-style possibilities, here's the science bit. Lighting can be divided into four key types, and a successful scheme usually marries them all. General lighting is just that—the central pendant, wall lights, recessed spots, and downlighters that create a basic level of illumination.

THIS PAGE *Lights can be practical or, as here, simply decorative. A string of fairy lights hanging around the entrance to a room softens its appearance and, when teamed with small mirror balls, sends pretty sparkles across the space. A striking glass chandelier beyond adds a more grown-up, classical feel.*

OPPOSITE LEFT *Rope lights can be fashioned into signs, creating an illuminated message. It's a kitsch but fun effect, and a strong feature in any room once evening comes.*

OPPOSITE RIGHT *The owners of this house made the contemporary-style sofa themselves and ran red rope lighting along its frame. When illuminated, the rope lights send a pinkish glow up behind the curtains hanging alongside.*

ABOVE LEFT *When the sun shines through the glass bricks in this Moroccan house, it is transformed into squares of color, cast across the floor.*

ABOVE RIGHT *An ordinary bulb inside a colored glass shade gives a soft, tinted light to a room.*

OPPOSITE, ABOVE LEFT *A lit votive softly illuminates the collectibles around it.*

OPPOSITE, ABOVE RIGHT *A rope light draped from this vase adds a warm glow to the cool marble of the fire surround.*

OPPOSITE, BELOW LEFT *Flower fairy lights illuminate this butterfly collection and mirror the design of the screen below.*

OPPOSITE, BELOW RIGHT *Fairy lights in an alcove create a relaxing glow, ideal for a bedroom.*

Task lighting helps with specific jobs, from writing to shaving. Examples include an Anglepoise desk lamp or the under-cabinet halogen spotlights in a kitchen. Accent light picks out a specific feature in a room and is about three times brighter than general light—think clip-on lights and spots that fit under shelves to show off a treasured ornament or collection. Natural light needs no introduction, but making the most of what we get is worthwhile.

Once you work out how each room will be used, choose a mix of light sources to create the right balance between ambience and practicality. You might also keep in mind a few simple tricks that can help make the most of a room's dimensions and features. Make a tall-ceilinged room feel cozier by clustering floor and table lamps together to create low pools of light and by installing

ABOVE LEFT *Painted silk lanterns bought in New York's Chinatown make a pretty hanging display —no need for lights inside.*

ABOVE RIGHT *Disks of hard, opaque capiz shell (a product of the oyster industry) are often used to make jewelry or, as here, elegant light shades. They make a pleasant tinkling sound when caught by the breeze.*

OPPOSITE LEFT *An arcing floor lamp with a dramatic globe shade makes a strong design statement in this living space, whether illuminated or not. Teamed with a striking table lamp on the console behind, the pair create flexible lighting that is bounced back into the room by the large wall mirror.*

OPPOSITE RIGHT *This Moroccan shade made of colored glass beads throws patterned light around the room and brings a touch of exoticism.*

downlighters, which send a wash of light down the walls and draw the eye away from the room's lofty proportions. To make a small room appear larger, position ceiling lights around the borders of the room, not just centrally. To maximize natural light, use minimal window treatments (fine voile curtains rather than thick velvet, for instance), hang mirrors opposite windows and work in lots of reflective surfaces and pale colors.

Once you have a good mix of light sources woven into your room and have decided where to position them, you're free to have fun with the decorative side of lighting. Beyond the simple drum shades typically fitted to lamps and pendants is a world of fanciful options, from curved plastic shades from the Sixties to tinkling capiz-shell pendants and painted paper lanterns. Each will give a simple light its own personality; each will influence

the amount of light that escapes into the room. A paper shade allows a mellow, even glow, while a perforated metal lantern from Morocco will send patterns across the walls. Mix and match shades and bases, particularly if you buy a standard fixture—give it a bazaar twist with a found shade, or customize a purchased shade by pinning on brooches, badges, and corsages.

As with furniture and collectibles, a bit of TLC can transform a tired secondhand lamp. Metal shades and gooseneck lights can be spray-painted, ceramic and glass bases can be cleaned with soapy water, and wooden bases can be painted. Lampshades, too, can be dusted and revamped by stitching on ribbons, buttons, or sequins. If you're buying secondhand, get the electrical fixture checked by an electrician, who can replace frayed cords or faulty bulb sockets inexpensively.

Lighting can be great fun to experiment with, and the bazaar look uses the more decorative, flexible types of modern lighting available to good effect. Rope lights, which are made of hundreds of LED lights inside a see-through cable, look great threaded up stairs or along a mantelpiece. Simple fairy lights come in a variety of colors and decorative shades, and create a pleasing ambient glow. Use them to pick out favorite pictures, thread them around a doorway, or wind them through logs in a fireplace.

When you tire of electric light, go back to nature with candles. From simple votives to delicate tapers, nothing beats the romance and beauty of a real flame. Better still, candles are cheap and widely available. The fun part is finding a home for them. From an old glass jar to an elaborate candelabra, there are endless ways to bring soft candlelight creatively into your home.

ABOVE *A Russian Impressionist painting gets an extra decorative twist with flower garlands and necklaces draped from its frame. It's a great way to enjoy your jewelry, too—much better than confining it to a box.*

RIGHT *Theming your displays of paintings is a useful technique when it comes to creating an impressive and cohesive wall of images. Here, kitsch "blue women" and other exotic ladies, all bought at London's Portobello Road market, cover one wall.*

OPPOSITE *Surrounded by framed pictures and photographs, this flat-screen TV, mounted on the wall, could easily be mistaken for a work of art.*

WALL ART

Finding pictures that suit your home and your style can be tricky if you limit your search to the mall, and not many of us have the budget to buy original pieces from galleries. The solution is to scour the secondhand market for oddities and one-offs that you love and will sit well in a bazaar-style home that's packed with unusual pieces. There's an abundance of old art and photography languishing in thrift stores and flea markets, often costing just a few dollars.

Take your pick, from amateur oil paintings and simple sketches to poignant family photographs of long-gone generations. Old metal advertising panels, touting everything from beer to soap, often crop up in flea markets. You will also find plenty of postcards from the early and mid-20th century, with photos or illustrations on the front. They all make great decoration for your walls, many boasting a twist of personal history that makes up for any amateurishness of technique or minor damage.

Mirrors are another wonderful addition to any room. Not only do they look great, but they also serve a practical purpose, helping to bounce light around, making the space feel brighter and bigger—hang a mirror opposite a window or door for maximum effect. They also create interesting optical tricks. Put a vase of flowers in front of a mirror and they look twice as lush. Position a row of flickering candles next to a mirror for double the glow. Mirrors come in all shapes and sizes. They can have a

THIS PAGE *Clothes can become art when carefully hung across a wall. Here, a collection of dresses and skirts, made by the fashion-designer owner of this house, lines one wall. If you display clothes this way, take them down regularly for a brush and shake out, to remove dust and prevent creases.*

OPPOSITE *Art for your walls does not need to be expensive. This corridor is lined with old magazine covers and fashion-shoot images, simply framed. In an adjoining room, embroidery scrolls showing birds, flowers, and oriental scenes are hung in a group to make a colorful contrast.*

flat or curved surface, be freestanding or wall-hung, framed with ornately carved wood or finished with a simple beveled edge. They suit pretty much any place in any room, since they are not bringing an image to the wall or surface on which they rest, merely reflecting the colors, light, and movement around them. Old mirrors can show their age. Brown spots may appear where the aluminum or silver that coats the glass to make it reflective has decayed and the reflection itself may have become misty, but both effects are attractive and testament to the age of the piece.

There are no rules to follow when displaying pictures and mirrors, but if you find yourself with an armful of images, a lot of blank walls, and no idea how to put the two together, take inspiration from the bazaars of Iran, Turkey, and Morocco.

Traditionally, large bazaars like Tehran's Grand Bazaar and the Covered Bazaar in Istanbul were split into corridors, each one specializing in certain types of goods, from spices and carpets to perfumes and precious metals. So use this rationale and group your images. Hang similar subjects together—portraits, landscapes, horses, still lifes of flowers—or paintings in the same medium, be that oil, charcoal, or watercolor. Or group them according to the color of the frame or the size of the image —a wall of large canvases can look striking, as can one peppered with an array of small photographs in neat black frames.

With the inspiration of real bazaars in mind, remember it is abundance and an organic quality that impresses, not neatness, so cover a wall with images dotted at random. Precision is not

THIS PAGE *A colorful patchwork canvas fills this chimney-breast wall. It is made from a collection of the patterned collars that Indian men traditionally wear at weddings, stitched together. Its tactile quality suits a bedroom, where sensuality and touchy-feely textiles are welcome.*

OPPOSITE LEFT *Bazaar style loves to tweak the conventional. Here, instead of arranging fresh flowers in a vase, they are casually taped to a wall to make a 3D artwork.*

OPPOSITE RIGHT *Photos, postcards, fake flowers, and magazine articles are pinned up to create a lively wall of images. It gives this workstation stacks of personality and visual interest, and it's practical, too—the more paperwork on the wall, the less there is cluttering the desk.*

LEFT *Religious imagery can look rather austere, but in this bedroom a holy image is softened by colorful embroidered quilts and pillows, scattered across the bed.*

OPPOSITE, ABOVE LEFT *A framed painting of a bird is kept company by three smaller images, creating a relaxed display.*

OPPOSITE, ABOVE RIGHT *A funky artwork by Takashi Murakami looks strong above this simple fire surround, while the patterned tiles look like small-scale paintings.*

OPPOSITE, BELOW LEFT *Whether you know the sitter or not, portraits make an arresting addition to any room. This is a portrait of the house's owner, painted by her ex-husband.*

OPPOSITE, BELOW RIGHT *This large, dramatic mirror adds a decorative blast to a white bathroom. Its shelf is home to sparkling jewelry and unusual collectibles, while everyday bathroom products are stored out of sight.*

essential, so don't worry about lining them up evenly—it is the overall impression that counts. Just mix and match images until you have a combination that pleases your eye. You can add to the arrangement as you find new ones or move them around as your preferences alter. The beauty of this kind of display, where many pictures are hung together, is that no single image has to be especially strong or eye-catching. You are free to pick up paintings and pictures of varying quality simply because they appeal to you—no need to hold out for a masterpiece.

Be resourceful, too. If you find a handsome frame with no image in it, use it to show off a family photograph, postcard, swatch of wallpaper, or fabric. Similarly, if you have unearthed an old oil painting without a frame, hang it as a plain canvas—it will look just as impressive. Seek out bargains, too. If you love mirrors, but your wallet won't stretch to the 19th-century French examples that are so popular today, why not collect beveled-edge mirrors from the Thirties and Forties? They are abundant and inexpensive. A quick surf on eBay or a wander around any flea

THIS PAGE *Made by the fashion-designer owner of this house, this canary-yellow gown makes a show-stopping piece of wall art. Combined with a matching vinyl-covered sofa and patterned pillows, it creates an uncompromisingly bright scheme.*

OPPOSITE LEFT *Hanging a mirror above a fireplace is a tried and tested look, but here the owner has had fun with the convention by choosing a small, oddly shaped mirror, which looks pleasingly quirky hung on a blank wall. Small Seventies paintings and a folk-art deer add color and further humor to this fireplace.*

OPPOSITE RIGHT *Bright colors in this painting are picked up in the flowers arranged in front.*

market should reveal several, and they look great hung in groups or propped along a mantelpiece or shelf.

A short time spent reviving old frames reaps rewards. Use a solution of mild detergent and warm water, a soft brush, and cotton cloth to ease off dust and grime. You could spray-paint a frame in striking gold or silver, or brush on a coat of eggshell to refresh it. Grimy glass and mirrors will regain their sparkle with some window cleaner, a soft dry cloth, and plenty of elbow grease.

As with every aspect of bazaar style, think laterally, too. Who says pictures need to be hung on walls? They can be appreciated just as well propped against a wall, or sitting on the floor, a chest of drawers, or a shelf. Team them with other pieces that you love, or give your picture an extra decorative touch by draping jewelry from its frame, stringing fairy lights around it, or tucking party invites or postcards between the frame and glass.

Finally, remember that wall art need not be confined to pictures and mirrors. Hang up beautiful vintage dresses, blouses, or skirts. Tape dried flowers to your walls. Pin up a throw, patchwork, or gorgeous blanket. Or release your inner Jackson Pollock and make your own mural.

COLLECTIBLES
and DISPLAY

Display is at the heart of bazaar style. It's a look that rejects the minimalist movement of the Eighties and Nineties and its obsession with hiding everything behind sleek cupboard doors. Instead, bazaar style celebrates the beauty of the things we gather up as we go through life, from family heirlooms to rummage-sale finds, vacation souvenirs to birthday gifts. Even those pieces not generally thought of as decorative can be arranged so we appreciate and enjoy them.

THIS PAGE *This beautiful cocktail cabinet on elegant legs is home to a selection of vodka bottles and a mixture of collectibles. From fake roses to jeweled necklaces, crystal decanters to pretty glasses, it's a showcase of interesting and delicate pieces, intended for permanent display and use— the doors are not meant to be shut. The mirrored back of the cupboard makes the collection seem twice as large.*

OPPOSITE *The windowsill in this Dutch home is covered with objects, some kitsch (a ceramic baby) and some traditional (the photo frames). Blankets and textiles are arranged on the bench in front to be enjoyed, too. Walls are kept plain to prevent the room from feeling too busy.*

THIS PAGE *An old display bust is a perfect place to hang necklaces, bangles, and garlands. This is a great example of how bazaar style takes the things we often clear away into boxes and pots and displays them creatively.*

OPPOSITE LEFT *This meeting of beautiful fine china and sparkling jewelry is pleasing to the eye but practical, too, as the teapot and cup are used to display and store the brooches, earrings, and necklaces.*

OPPOSITE RIGHT *These clothes look too good to be hidden behind closet doors. Hung from an ornate mirror, they add glamour and color to this bedroom. The mirror and drawers were found in a thrift shop and repainted in pastel shades.*

When it comes to what you display, the choice is vast. From tin tea caddies to earthenware cider kegs, from colored tumblers to costume jewelry, collectibles are everywhere. By far the easiest bazaar-style pieces to source, they are fun, often inexpensive, and gloriously abundant. In any flea market, garage sale, or home accessories store you've ever been into, collectibles make up the vast bulk of pieces on sale. And, although you may be looking for a particular item, you're just as likely to see something else that takes your fancy, finding yourself drawn to it for a variety of reasons—nostalgia, sensuality, color, or texture. Trust your instincts and go with your heart. If it's a pineapple ice bucket from the Sixties that appeals to you that day, snap it up—you're sure to find a space in your home for it. Genuine enthusiasm for the object is all that matters.

While they can deliver years of pleasure, collectibles also offer instant gratification. Furniture can take time to hunt down or need repairs to be usable. Curtains might need to be altered. Wallpaper must be hung. But collectibles bring an instant lift to any room by their presence alone. Team them with other similar pieces to boost a collection, or let them stand alone to be fully appreciated. Either way, there's little work involved in gaining enjoyment from a collectible—you only have to look at it.

Collectibles aren't just those pieces intended as ornaments. Almost anything can take on collectible status. From the kitchen, old pickle jars and soda bottles, painted flasks, or biscuit tins can look lovely grouped together and are easy to find at markets and thrift stores. Pieces with a practical purpose, from egg cups to teapots, canisters to cookie cutters, can be decorative, too, so

when you're not using them, display them on open shelves. Non-domestic sources like laboratories, department stores, schools, and hospitals shed their excess baggage over the years, and it often washes up on the shores of secondhand stores. You might find apothecary jars, scales, globes, cameras, clocks, registers, keys, and weights. These can all look decorative, displayed alone or casually sitting amid a muddle of other well-loved pieces.

Have your bazaar-style radar on when you're abroad, too. The quality and variety of contemporary homewares in overseas shops, particularly in Europe, can be incredibly high, and adding an impressive modern piece to a group of found objects can bring freshness and vigor to a display. Similarly, the injection of some ethnic artefacts or artisan-made pieces will sit well with older

ABOVE LEFT *Giving your displays a loose theme can help to create visual cohesion. Here, candlesticks and glassware sit together on top of a cupboard, catching the light.*

ABOVE RIGHT *Decorative Indian candlesticks, arranged in an alcove, don't need to be topped with lighted candles to look beautiful. A jeweled curtain hanging behind adds light and sparkle to the space and frames the display.*

OPPOSITE *Filling a corner of your home with fresh flowers in a mix of brightly patterned, different-height vases creates a strong impact. Here, the blooms and their decorative vessels add welcome color to the gray-painted hutch and walls.*

finds and secondhand oddments back home, so hit the markets, bazaars, and even hardware stores in countries like Turkey and India for good-looking, well-made gear, from woven baskets and metal lunch boxes to colorful tea glasses and plates.

When it comes to displaying your collectibles, play around with the objects you have, trying out different groupings until you find a mix that pleases. One of the delights of bazaar style rests in giving unusual pieces a center-stage position; in teaming the conventional with the curious, the simple with the ornate. Theming your displays can help. Glass bottles and vases, metal tins and pots, black-and-white pieces—the possibilities are endless. Make your theme narrow (flower-patterned teacups), or broad (any item of silverware); whatever your approach, this method will help you sort through your collectibles and find harmonious ways of displaying them.

An extension of this thematic approach is to create a collection purposefully, hunting down ceramics from a particular pottery, maker, or area, for example, or gathering specific items, from salt and pepper shakers to brass candlesticks. The added bonus to this approach is that it makes every trip to a market, fair, or interiors shop more exciting—the thrill of finding another piece for your collection is great. Looking for a specific item or class of item gives direction to your search, too, helping you to navigate your way through the sea of objects laid out on each stand.

While it's fun to create collections or themed displays, it's the innate flexibility of collectibles that is so appealing. So, once you have a display established, don't sit back and let it stagnate. Remember to add to it, move its components around, or swap them with pieces from another room. Put some items away in a cupboard, hiding them for a few months so you can enjoy them

afresh when you reintroduce them to a room. Forget buying a new chair or repainting the walls; rearranging your collectibles is the fastest way to give a room a facelift—and it costs nothing.

To help show off your finds, choose open shelves, glass-fronted cabinets, and hutches. Decorative side tables will give you space to create small arrangements. Look out, too, for those more unusual pieces that are a good shape to show off specific collections. A dressmaker's mannequin could be draped with your favorite necklaces or a vintage dress, a huge bowl could hold an assortment of colorful doorknobs or pretty pebbles.

Rethink every room of your house, too. No space is too small for a cluster of objects. In fact, making an unusual location or forgotten corner home to a handful of pieces brings it to life. The unexpected pleasure of seeing a pretty object in an overlooked nook makes you appreciate it all the more. Glass

ABOVE LEFT *Black, white, and gray appear in the cabinet these collectibles are arranged on and on the pieces themselves, for a display that's easy on the eye.*

ABOVE RIGHT *Painting shelves the same color as the wall they hang against is a clever way to make the collectibles on them stand out, or—as with the pieces on the bottom shelf—almost disappear.*

OPPOSITE LEFT *Picture frames and, as here, the glass-fronted door of a cabinet are good places to tuck a photo or postcard.*

OPPOSITE RIGHT *This jewelry is too pretty to hide away and instead takes on a display role by being draped over a dressing-table mirror.*

ABOVE LEFT *A collection of ceramic salt and pepper shakers and china banks, arranged on curvy, contemporary shelves, brings further color to this orange-painted kitchen. They were picked up in secondhand shops, fairs, and flea markets by the owner.*

ABOVE RIGHT *A collection of vases sits neatly on this mantelpiece. Turning three of them onto their sides, so the tops face out, creates additional visual variety. The colors in the vases are echoed in the warm sunshine of the painting above, to tie this display together.*

votive holders can perch on top of window frames, a string of fake flowers can hang from a doorknob, a row of printer's letters can stand above a door frame.

Whatever the mix of collectibles, remember to season it with plenty of humor. Bazaar style doesn't take itself too seriously and is all about having fun with your home's interior. Collectibles are a great way to introduce some frivolity into your rooms. Pieces that are over-the-top ornate, luridly colored, or simply incredibly dated can all seem amusing now, while a quirky combination can bring humor to a single piece that, left alone, might not look so appealing. An old stone bust gets a witty new look when topped with a trilby; a slightly naff figurine looks splendid draped with bangles or sporting a fantastic feather hat. Not everyone will appreciate the joke, but that doesn't mean it isn't funny!

ABOVE *Positioning this figure of a kneeling angel, which could look rather serious on its own, above a shelf of colorful woven baskets and handbags gives it lightness and warmth.*

LEFT *Mantelpieces are ideal places to have fun with display. Figurines, busts, candlesticks, giant letters—they look great together and can be moved around easily to refresh the look. A table spread with candy, cakes, and chocolates, in glass vases and stands, completes the relaxed, unpretentious feel of this dining space.*

THIS PAGE *A small alcove in this Moroccan house is the perfect place to install shelves and create an eye-catching display. A collection of Indian artefacts creates a splash of color and exoticism in a simply furnished dining space.*

OPPOSITE, ABOVE LEFT *The clear design and strong colors on this coffee pot and milk jug are typical hallmarks of Seventies ceramics.*

OPPOSITE, ABOVE RIGHT *Colored tea glasses and bowls look beautiful on glass shelves, illustrating how everyday items deserve to be displayed—an idea central to bazaar style.*

OPPOSITE, BELOW LEFT *Even the humble mug or glass—kitchen essentials—can look fantastic when casually stacked on a shelf.*

OPPOSITE, BELOW RIGHT *A collection of metal canisters with bird designs looks highly decorative when grouped together, but has a practical purpose, too, holding kitchen gear and cooking ingredients.*

rooms

THIS PAGE *White walls and flooring create a simple, clean backdrop for this eating space, allowing the collection of paintings to stand out. Old French-style dining chairs with rush seats are brought up to date with brightly colored cushions, while the table remains neutral, thanks to a crisp white cloth with delicate embroidery.*

OPPOSITE *There's an organic feel to the cooking space in this Moroccan home, thanks to the built-in sink, work surface, and shelving, made of solid material then rendered to look exactly like the room's walls. Cooking implements are on display and in easy reach, but there's space for some eye-catching artwork on the lofty walls, too.*

COOKING
and EATING SPACES

Cooking and eating used to be two very separate activities. The kitchen was a functional place where food was prepared, while meals were taken in the dining room. Nowadays, with space at a premium and our passion for open-plan living strong, many homes have combined the two areas. Today's busy families and confident cooks prefer to gather in one place to eat, chat, work, and relax.

THIS PAGE AND OPPOSITE LEFT *This spacious Amsterdam apartment has a large cooking and eating space where friends and family can comfortably gather. The refectory-style tables are made from recycled lumber. The green seats are Robin Day's Polo chair, designed in 1975 as a variation on his classic stacking Polyprop chair. The exposed pipework on the ceiling and simple contemporary kitchen units give the space an industrial air, which is softened by the colorful china, glass, and baskets dotted around the space. On one wall, fresh flowers are stuck using black tape—an unexpected and amusing way to display your blooms.*

OPPOSITE RIGHT *Stack up colored glasses on shelves for a beautiful, simple display. Group matching colors together to create a bold effect.*

Combining eating and cooking spaces is practical—everything is on hand, from china to condiments—and sociable, too. What cook wants to be isolated in a back room while their friends relax in the living room? There's also something about the warmth, good smells, color, and activity of a cooking space that draws us to it. Add a table and chairs and it will become the hub of the home.

With its laidback vibe and emphasis on display, the bazaar look suits this informal, communal way of living. Plates, glasses, and flatware are stored on open shelves—no need for friends to ask where to find them. A hodgepodge of flatware, gathered over the years, sets a relaxed tone, and it can be stored in a simple basket on the table, readily at hand when people gather for a meal. Fabric remnants make pretty tablecloths, old linen tea towels make oversized napkins, comfy cushions soften a bench and jelly jars are ideal for holding flowers for the table. It's a look that instantly puts people at ease and invites friends to unwind.

ABOVE LEFT *Tea served from pretty china cups, ornate candlesticks, chocolate truffles arranged on old glass cake stands—a bazaar-style dining space is attractive, relaxing, and quirky.*

ABOVE RIGHT *When hung along a wall or arranged thoughtfully on a shelf, kitchen utensils and gear can look beautiful.*

The bazaar-style cooking and eating space is easy on your wallet, too. There is no need to splash out on matching dining chairs from a chain store when a mix of thrift-store chairs or a couple of benches will look wonderful. Alternatively, if you lose your heart to a set of modern classics—Saarinen's Tulip chairs or Panton's S chairs, for example—you can economize on the table, choosing a secondhand model that needs a lick of paint or topping basic trestles with a sheet of toughened glass.

Similarly, by opting for deliberately mismatched china, it's cheap and easy to amass a set large enough to cater for a crowd. Just pick up the components of a dinner service as and when you see them, perhaps sticking to a theme, like floral patterns or

built-in units. Cooking spaces today are often high-tech, high-cost temples to efficiency and hygiene, packed with machines and gadgets, but lacking personality. They are one area of the home in which we often stifle our creative instincts, preferring strong lines, sleek units, and tough materials such as stainless steel over the more colorful and sensual styles we would choose for other rooms. Modern kitchens can cost a small fortune, too, becoming more of a status symbol than a relaxed place to cook and eat. However, it doesn't have to be that way. Bazaar style

encourages a less designed, more organic approach to fitting out our cooking and eating spaces. Why not choose a few pieces of handsome old furniture instead? Armoires, cupboards, glass-fronted cabinets, and hutches can hold the bulk of your cookware and dishes, and in a good-sized room you can rely on one big table as your work surface—no need to fit expensive counters.

If using old furniture that was never intended for life in a kitchen seems a step too far, consider using secondhand kitchen units or furniture instead. Don't be afraid to ask if you

Meal

THIS PAGE *A neat dining space opens off the cooking area in this Moroccan house. A classic Saarinen Tulip dining table is surrounded by retro chairs with a slightly beaten-up look, creating a relaxed modern feel. The lampshade is made from capiz shells.*

OPPOSITE LEFT *Covering a wallpapered wall with clear plastic is an easy way to give a stylish modern kitchen a bazaar feel and create a practical, wipe-clean backsplash at the same time. Vivid orange walls and retro collectibles prevent those chic new units looking too clinical, too.*

OPPOSITE RIGHT *The dark paneled walls of this dining space are given extra drama with plenty of orange tones and retro furniture. The glass-topped dining table, molded chairs, and sculptural candlesticks are all retro classics.*

can salvage units from dumpsters, or check your local paper or eBay for them. You may only want to buy a couple, not a whole kitchen's worth, to supplement other freestanding pieces, but this is often possible. You may be lucky and track down some vintage units, too. Kitchen cupboards from the Fifties are highly desirable and very stylish, while individual cupboards from the Forties or Fifties often crop up at markets, complete with frosted sliding doors and melamine finish. Remember to be resourceful, too. If you love the unit, but don't like its finish, remember that

you can paint it. Specialized furniture and cupboard paint transforms old melamine in one coat and comes in a range of colors. Alternatively, cover the doors with wallpaper to give them a fresh, informal makeover.

Bazaar-style cooking spaces often combine built-in with freestanding furniture, to get the best of both worlds. You could line one wall with built-in units and a contemporary sink, then find the remaining storage at markets and fairs. Or have a run of open units made from bricks or concrete, and fill them with

THIS PAGE *This vast ceramic sink was a salvage yard find.*

OPPOSITE *Design classics like Eero Saarinen's Tulip table and chairs, designed in 1957, work well in a bazaar-style home. Teamed with older pieces of furniture like the console table and a mixed collection of vases, pots, and lights, their clean modern lines are softened, but still act as a fresh contrast to the ornate carving and delicate details of their room mates. The huge mirror is an old Venetian piece, bought in New York by the previous owners of this house. When they came to sell their home, they decided it was too heavy and fragile to move, and left it for the next owners, who happened to be friends of theirs, to enjoy.*

baskets to house your food and kitchenware. If you're handy with a hammer, or know a man who can, make your own units using reclaimed wood for a rustic, cottagey feel. You could even ditch the doors and string a curtain across the front—a great way to casually conceal large appliances such as the washing machine, too. Another smart alternative is to buy inexpensive cabinet carcasses from a home-dec warehouse, then have a carpenter make the doors to your specification. Whatever you do, think creatively and resist the urge to equip your cooking space with uniform built-in units from one supplier. A mix of new, old, and reclaimed furniture will bring stacks more personality to the space, and when well planned it will function efficiently, too.

While it is possible to fit out your eating space completely with recycled or secondhand furniture, an up-to-date oven and fridge are a must for all but the most peripatetic of cooks. There's no need to opt for run-of-the-mill white goods, though. There are several Fifties-style fridges on the market, including Smeg's FAB design, that are good-looking enough to become a real feature of any cooking or dining space. Freestanding ovens, once the preserve of rented apartments, are now state of the art and much loved by serious cooks, as are modern ranges. Their unfitted nature suits a kitchen with odd angles and dimensions. They sit well in a chimney breast, for example, becoming a modern-day version of the ancient hearth.

For all your other kitchen essentials, head to classic bazaar-style sources—salvage yards, secondhand fairs, flea markets. Old ceramic sinks (also called butler's sinks) can turn up at reclamation yards and cost far less than their new equivalents. They may not have a pristine white finish, but any crazing (cracking in the glaze) adds to their character, and there is no difference in installation or plumbing methods between a brand-new and a reclaimed sink. Although incredibly strong, they can be chipped if hit at the wrong angle by something hard such as a heavy pan, but don't let minor damage put you off. Repair kits for filling and sealing chips are available from specialists.

Lighting is another cooking-space essential, and here a mix of contemporary and reclaimed can work very well. Task lighting is essential in a kitchen. Slicing meat and chopping vegetables become perilous activities in a poorly lit room, while washing dishes and cooking are frustrating when you can't see what you're

doing properly. Installing modern spotlights under units or using ceiling spots that can be directed so you don't cast a shadow over your work is prudent. The halogen bulbs used in spotlights provide a clear, bright light that is not as warm and yellow as traditional tungsten filament bulbs—ideal for working with.

Once task lighting is in place, you can add ambient lighting for mealtimes and socializing. A row of pendant lights or lanterns hung over a long table adds drama and creates a strong focal point. Small lamps on the table or shelves will also contribute to a soft light. Don't forget candles, either. It's amazing how a table strewn with papers and keys can be transformed into a magical place for a relaxing meal by a sprinkling of candles and votives—minimal clearing up required.

If your home already boasts a contemporary kitchen, there are plenty of ways to give it a bazaar feel. Rather than stash all your pans and dishes away, bring them out so you can enjoy their

THIS PAGE *This outdoor dining space in Morocco looks calm and elegant, thanks to a fuss-free scheme of white and pink. A sturdy whitewashed table is flanked by white cushions on a built-in bench and wooden chairs. It makes a fresh backdrop for a mix of pretty pink plates and bowls and simple glasses, all made of plastic and bought in a local market.*

OPPOSITE LEFT *Why serve sugar from a box when it can find a home in this gorgeous lidded bowl? Plastic tableware like this is cheap and available in any Moroccan market.*

OPPOSITE RIGHT *Although it has a practical use, this pink flask is beautiful, too, and looks lovely displayed next to fresh flowers.*

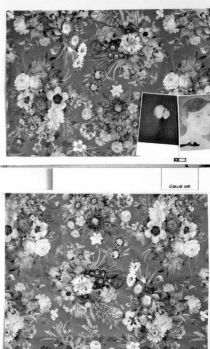

THIS PAGE *Pasting wallpaper to tired kitchen units and a plain white fridge is an inspired—and inexpensive—way to give them a colorful new look. Although it looks like an old-fashioned design, this paper was recently bought at a home-dec warehouse.*

OPPOSITE *A deep windowsill in this Dutch apartment is used to house a display of plates and other collectibles. The table, too, is home to unusual vases, and the bare plaster wall is given a humorous lift with a cow-head sculpture, sporting hat, bag, and feathers.*

various colors and shapes. Fit shelves on a blank wall or replace some of the solid unit doors with glass so you can see the cupboard contents. Hang saucepans from butcher's hooks on a chain or metal grid fixed to the wall. Add paintings, photos, or some vibrant wallpaper. Create a colorful backsplash using reclaimed tiles, or wallpaper protected behind clear plastic or reinforced glass. Inject some color and have fun—even the most neutral modern units and countertops can become full of personality when you work a little bazaar-style magic.

THIS PAGE *Colorful artwork, squashy cushions in vibrant shades, plenty of textiles and throws layered over comfy sofas—this living room marries comfort, style, and individuality seamlessly.*

OPPOSITE *White floorboards and walls unite a living space that flows into a dining area. The open-plan space is given further cohesion by patterns, textiles, and colors that don't match, but do share a vibrancy and brilliance. Pinks, reds, and oranges in particular crop up throughout the scheme.*

LIVING SPACES

Your living space might be the busy heart of the
home, or a tranquil haven. It could be the biggest
room in your house, or an intimate snug corner.
It may flow, open-plan style, into an eating and
cooking space, or be completely separate from the
rest of your home. For that reason, it needs to be
flexible and well planned, but personal, too.
Bazaar style can deliver all this—and more.

Your living room can perform a host of different functions. You may use it as a place to socialize, read, watch TV, relax, work, or all of those things. Once you have identified how you will be using your living space, you can easily plan how to work in color, lighting, furniture, and window treatments that will be fit for purpose and bursting with bazaar style.

Think about the walls first—a room's biggest backdrops. Bazaar style's emphasis on displaying objects means that it's often an easy and smart option to keep walls neutral. Let your collectibles, rugs, furniture, and artwork bring in the color, texture, and pattern. Off-white is a safe choice, but avoid brilliant white, which contains optical brighteners that produce a blue tone, making it look cold and harsh. There are hundreds of off-whites to choose from; use several for a layered effect. You could also leave plaster walls bare or brickwork exposed. If you

yearn to bring color onto your walls, remember that dark shades will make a space feel smaller, while light will make it feel bigger.

After the walls, floors are the biggest surface in any room. A living space sees a fair amount of traffic, so it needs a hard-wearing surface, but it is also a place of relaxation, so something aesthetically pleasing and kind to bare feet is necessary, too. Wooden floors are a good bet. Wood is attractive, practical, and fairly tough without being cold. If you're lucky enough to find good-quality boards hiding beneath a grotty carpet, just clean them with a solution of one part turpentine, one part methylated spirits, and one part vinegar before treating them with a sealant. If some of the boards are rotten, add replacement boards. Find a good match at a reclamation yard, or piece in new wood and hide it beneath a rug. If you're after a more uniform finish, paint your boards. Dark colors will cover a multitude of knots and

THIS PAGE *Black floorboards won't make a room seem dark. Instead, they provide a strong backdrop for furniture and finds. A neutral sofa and armchair are invigorated with an embroidered throw from India and striped cushions from Morocco. The painted wooden chest doubles as storage and a place to rest a drink or book. The foil and glass painting is by Helen O'Keefe.*

OPPOSITE LEFT *Fresh flowers are an instant and natural way to add color to even the smallest space.*

OPPOSITE RIGHT *Shelves fitted in an alcove can hold much more than books. Photos, collectibles, and lamps can all find a home here, creating little framed tableaux.*

THIS PAGE AND OPPOSITE *This airy living space in an Amsterdam house has turned its back on the traditional idea that a sofa and armchairs are essential. Instead, there's a relaxed, North African feel to the room, with low-level seating, floor cushions, and tables, all from Morocco, where the owner also has a home. Choosing this kind of seating over a sofa has the added advantage of making the room feel bigger and less cluttered—no bulky furniture in here. A bright scheme of yellow and green looks great—a large space can handle strong color—while exposed brickwork and bare plaster by the huge picture window add a pleasing roughness to this colorful, well-ordered room.*

blemishes, and if the boards are already reasonably smooth you may not need to sand them—the paint will even out small imperfections. Alternatively, lay new boards, which are available in a huge choice of woods, widths, and finishes.

Wall-to-wall carpet has fallen out of favor in recent decades, especially in busy downstairs rooms, so if you have hard floors but still crave carpet's soft feel underfoot, work in a selection of rugs. Toe-tickling sheepskin, animal hides, fluffy flokatis, colorful Moroccan mats—there's plenty of choice. Rugs often show up at markets and fairs. If they look a bit grubby, remember

they can be professionally cleaned (or just dry-cleaned if small enough), and don't be put off by a little wear—it adds to the relaxed, bazaar feel. You can also create a rug by having a carpet offcut edged. Called whipping, this service is reasonably priced. Look out for rugs when you go abroad, too, but be careful when buying animal hides. They are often "raw," which means they won't wear well—or smell great. Check that the hide has been professionally tanned before buying.

Rugs can be as striking as a piece of art, but they also have a practical function, deadening the sound of footsteps and

THIS PAGE *Fascinating retro and secondhand glass, metallic, and plexiglass pieces fill this airy living space. The owner found the white cube in a secondhand shop and added black spots to transform it into a dice side table. The leather sofa came from an antiques fair, and the metal storage is an old French school locker.*

OPPOSITE LEFT *This cute sideboard was found in a thrift shop. The zebra came from a secondhand market in England, where the owner also has a booth and sells the vintage wallpaper that's standing in the box here.*

OPPOSITE RIGHT *Black and white ceramics are naturally at home alongside black-and-white photographs in monochrome frames.*

softening and warming a hard floor. They can influence the impression of space, too. Run striped rugs across a room to make it feel wider, or down a room to make it appear longer. You can also use them to zone a multipurpose space. For example, a large rug can define the living area in an open-plan layout when you position it under a sofa, coffee table, and seating. If a corner of your living room is a place of work, demarcate the work zone by laying a rug under the desk.

When you're picking a rug, you can be bolder in your choice of pattern and color than you would be with carpet, because you can move it easily and a rug is not such a large investment as carpet. You might even want to roll up your rugs and pack them

LEFT *There's a patchwork theme to this living space. Two Chesterfield-style sofas have been recovered in a mix of colorful patterned fabrics, which the owner had been collecting for years. She found the bulk of it in a secondhand shop in England. It could look chaotic, but closer inspection reveals that the same fabrics have been used on the same parts of each sofa. This patchwork mix looks glorious and is an inexpensive way to recover a sofa, as anything from old curtains to fabric remnants can be used, picked up in markets, fabric stores, or on eBay. The chimney breast is decorated in the same way, but with wallpaper samples. Neutral walls and a wooden floor anchor the look, while matching lamps, either side of the fire, add symmetry and balance.*

away for summer, or swap shag pile for simple mats when the weather gets warm. Pattern on rugs is a good idea because it hides marks better than a plain finish. Remember that big patterns can act as a focal point, mid-scale patterns provide a degree of visual interest, while small-scale patterns add overall texture.

Living rooms work best when they have a focal point, so before you start positioning your furniture figure out what that is. Realistically, it's often the TV, so arrange some seating for viewing it comfortably. Position the rest of your seating at an angle or even facing away from the screen, to encourage other activities such as reading. Traditionally, the focal point in a living room was the fireplace. If yours is unattractive, seek out a handsome original from a salvage yard. The mantelpiece itself can become a fantastic bazaar-style focal point, dotted with your favorite collectibles. Hang a mirror or painting above it, or use wallpaper or a different paint color to give the chimney breast maximum impact. If the fireplace is a working one, so much the better. No one can resist cozying around a fire on a chilly night. Arrange seating close to it to enjoy the warmth, but be aware of the view from the door—a row of seat backs looks unwelcoming.

Seating is crucial to any living space. Most living spaces work best with a mix of one or two sofas and a few armchairs and

THIS PAGE *There are some pieces of classic modern design in this living space, including the Lansdowne sofa by Terence Woodgate (from SCP), the Tribeca coffee table by Noguchi, designed in 1944, and the rug by Marni for The Rug Company. They are given a bazaar-style feel through the patterned curtains, quirky Indian throw pillows, and small display of collectibles by the window. It's the difference between this being a sleek modern room and a bazaar-style room.*

OPPOSITE LEFT *A hallway is a great place to showcase a knock-out chandelier. So often a neglected part of the house, the hall is much used every day and deserves a little decoration.*

OPPOSITE RIGHT *Two armchairs sit opposite the red sofa (seen on this page), while the boldly patterned Marni rug helps to zone the space and tie it together.*

chairs. If you're buying a secondhand sofa or armchair, check that the frame is strong and the padding adequate. Having either resprung and restuffed is expensive, so if necessary get a quote before you buy. But if its only fault is a dilapidated cover, this can be hidden under throws, sheepskins, and blankets.

When it comes to chairs, bazaar-style classics include Lloyd Loom chairs, made from twisted paper reinforced with steel wire, stackable chairs with colorful plastic seats, squashy armchairs recovered in vibrant fabric, and the humble dining chair in all its manifestations, from a solid farmhouse number in painted pine to a curvaceous modernist example with tubular steel frame and leather seat. A row of theater seats (look in salvage yards),

a low bench or pew, wooden stools, or a leather pouffe would also look at home. If your room is small, remember that sofas or armchairs that sit on legs will make it feel bigger, because you can see beneath them a little way. Although seating is generally freestanding, don't rule out building some in. A carpenter can create a low platform along one wall or in a bay window or alcove, which you can pad with square cushions.

Don't forget the windows when you're styling your living space. The right window treatment offers privacy by night, without blocking out precious natural light by day. Heavy curtains will help insulate your room in winter, while fine voile can be drawn across to mask an uninspiring view or give some privacy,

THIS PAGE *Wooden cupboard doors and parquet flooring give this room in a Moroccan riad a warmth that's enhanced with splashes of orange on the throw across the sofa, the woven chair, and the fresh roses. A tinkling capiz-shell lampshade works well in this high-ceilinged space—a smaller shade could look lost in a room with such lofty dimensions—and adds some decoration and sparkle to this simply furnished corner.*

OPPOSITE, LEFT AND RIGHT *A wall of colored glass bricks makes an unusual partition in this living space, separating it slightly from the dining area beyond. A brilliant vase is filled with colored feathers—a non-wilting alternative to flowers that pack just as pretty a punch.*

while still allowing light to filter through. Remember that direct sunlight can bleach a strong color in a matter of months, so if your room faces south consider shades that can be rolled up completely to protect them from the sun's powerful rays, or choose curtains in a pale color that won't fade so obviously.

Natural light is invaluable in any room. Maximize it by installing curtain rods that extend well beyond the window frame, so you can pull curtains clear of the window. Use pretty silk scarves or colorful ribbon as simple tiebacks. Paint windowsills white and keep them clutter-free, then work in some reflective surfaces near the window—a fringe of glass beads sewn to the curtain edges can catch the sun, creating a little sparkle and increasing the brightness. If you prefer blinds, rollers do not block out light when completely up, unlike Roman shades, which will always obscure the top quarter of the window.

Flea markets and rummage sales come up trumps when you're hunting for old curtains. Launder them in a washing

ABOVE LEFT *A Moroccan beaded wedding blanket has been used here to cover cushions and some built-in seating, giving it an exotic feel. Reflective sequins in the fabric catch the light from the window, creating a little sparkle and boosting light levels.*

ABOVE RIGHT *Concrete floors can be painted with floor paint, which comes in a range of colors. A deep red was used here. On the wall behind this elegant chair, disparate images are pinned up casually to create a low-level display. The white chair in the background is La Chaise, by Charles and Ray Eames.*

OPPOSITE *Dark, almost sinister paintings are balanced with some brightness via the floral cushions and reflective glassware on the console table.*

THIS PAGE *Low-level built-in seating like this is typical of Moroccan homes, but easy to replicate. Cushions are essential to keep it comfortable—these are covered with a Moroccan wedding blanket.*

OPPOSITE, ABOVE LEFT *A wall of simple shelves creates lots of room to display favorite collectibles. These vases pick out the green of the armchair and white of the walls.*

OPPOSITE, ABOVE RIGHT *Two big, comfy armchairs have been recovered in a patchwork of pretty vintage fabrics.*

OPPOSITE, BELOW LEFT *These unusual old chairs sit beautifully in a big bay window area. A child's ferris wheel toy adds some color and frivolity to the white room.*

OPPOSITE, BELOW RIGHT *An upstairs landing is an ideal place to paste patterned wallpaper, giving this often overlooked part of a home some personality.*

machine—you may have to use one of the giant-drummed machines in a laundromat—and factor some fabric shrinkage into your measurements. Keep your eyes peeled for fabric that could be made into a curtain or blind, too—a length of vintage lace, voile, or sari fabric, a tablecloth or bedspread. Hunt down lengths of old monogrammed linen and have them made into Roman shades, string up a beaded curtain, stick sheets of colored film to the glass, or get a handyman to build simple shutters that will fold back completely against the wall. Hiding within those plain panes is a bazaar-style window trying to get out.

When you're adding the finishing touches to your living room—the extra bits of furniture or decoration—look out for pieces that appeal to you, whatever room they were originally intended for. A metal patio table can work just as well in a living room as on a deck; a chest of drawers need not live in the bedroom. Choose a mix of large pieces that will need to sit tight once positioned, and lightweight, flexible items—low tables, stools, baskets, storage boxes, screens—that can be moved around, both to refresh the room and to facilitate its different roles. If you're short on space, find pieces that can multitask. Old metal trunks or leather suitcases can work as low tables and storage, holding everything from toys to newspapers.

Remember, any piece can be given a bazaar-style revamp. Clean it, paint it, wallpaper it, pepper it with pretty finds, or drape it with patterned textiles. Top a simple unit or table with a sheet of patterned wallpaper, covered with glass cut to fit. Give

a display cabinet extra impact by installing mirrored glass behind the shelves—your favorite collectibles will look twice as good. Keep the look alive by adding, subtracting, mixing, and matching. A bazaar-style living space is constantly evolving.

The work space in your home may just be a place where you catch up on paperwork, or you may spend sizeable chunks of your day there. It might be a separate room, or part of a living space or bedroom. Either way, most of us manage little more than some colorful Post-it notes by way of decoration in this crucial area.

Add in some functional office furniture and you have the makings of an uninspiring space. It need not be so. The principles of bazaar style can be applied to a work area just as they can to a bedroom or kitchen, with equally pleasing results.

Let's begin with the desk. Rather than rushing to the nearest furniture warehouse for something practical but dull, try flea markets, thrift shops, and even salvage yards, for a desk that is functional and attractive. A small kitchen table with folding sides will fit even the snuggest of spaces, while a reclamation yard

THIS PAGE AND OPPOSITE RIGHT *A chunky old table, secondhand office chair, and a good-sized cupboard are the raw materials of any work space. Here, a gooseneck lamp helps illuminate the sewing machine for close work, while the window provides a good level of natural light. The wall behind the table is decorated with handkerchiefs, which the apartment's owner has embroidered with news headlines.*

OPPOSITE LEFT *Dressmaking patterns are pinned to the wall in this fashion designer's home.*

THIS PAGE *For dressmaking or needlework, a large table is useful, providing a surface to spread fabric out on. This table is made of old wooden crates and scaffolding poles.*

OPPOSITE LEFT *This lovely old desk has been painted white to soften its appearance. Drawers and cupboards provide storage for paperwork, leaving the surface clear for a few pretty pieces. Instead of a heavy, unattractive office chair, an old dining chair does the job and fits in well. Simple Venetian blinds hung at the window offer some privacy and help diffuse the light.*

OPPOSITE RIGHT *A simple kitchen table is the perfect size for a laptop and suits this small-scale home office. An attractive lamp and window shade keep the room fresh.*

might offer an old workbench or school lab table that would make an excellent workstation.

For seating, pick up a swivel office chair at a flea market, or make do with a simple dining chair or folding patio chair that can be tucked away when not in use. Then keep an eye out for office castoffs that can find a new home in your work space. Old map chests with their numerous drawers offer plentiful storage, while metal filing cabinets can be sanded down and spray-painted to lose their traditional gray finish. Storage boxes, shelves, drawer units, gooseneck lamps—all kinds of useful work-space gear is languishing in a market or thrift shop near you.

Work spaces need to be visually stimulating and inspiring without being cluttered, so function and form must combine. A bulletin board can hold all your notes and invitations, while becoming an attractive artwork, too. For a larger display, line a wall with cork tiles (which can be painted), or apply blackboard paint to one section for the daily to-do list. Always sniff around for an attractive alternative to the mundane. Pencils need not be stored in a dull plastic container; they can live in jugs or mason jars. Mesh letter trays can be replaced with shallow wooden crates or wire baskets. Think laterally to make your work space good-looking, but hard-working, too.

THIS PAGE *You can't beat a roll-top bathtub for glamour. The underside of this one is painted olive green, a color picked out in the rug, mirror frame, and floorboards. An old occasional table is just the right height to stand next to it, holding a candelabra and fresh flowers.*

OPPOSITE *Bathrooms can be home to all kinds of furniture, chosen for its practicality and good looks. Here, an ornate stand holds towels, while a peg rail, usually found in a hall, is home to bathtime essentials. A colorful rug softens the white-painted floorboards. The lampshade is made from old tins, with holes punched in, bought in Morocco.*

BATHING SPACES

Bazaar-style bathrooms, just like kitchens, don't need to be high-tech or sleek. They can be a mix of the reclaimed and the new, vintage and contemporary. So for a beautiful bathing space with heaps of personality, just give it the classic bazaar-style treatment, displaying daily essentials creatively, mixing in plenty of color, pattern, and texture and tweaking convention here and there. Sofa by the bath, anyone?

The idea of a room in every home dedicated to personal hygiene and grooming is, strictly speaking, a recent one. Most houses built before 1900 didn't have bathrooms, so in just 100 years the bathroom has evolved from a luxury novelty to a universal fixture in the modern home. We've also changed our attitude to them. From seeing bathrooms as a place for a quick wash and brush-up—a functional, often cramped room—we now want our bathing spaces to be sanctuaries. We go there to retreat from the world, locking the door to unwind and rejuvenate. Whether it's a soak in a bath at the end of the day or a peaceful primp as you prepare for work, we expect them to blend practicality with personal style.

Bazaar style works brilliantly in a bathing space, no matter what raw materials—the tub, sink, and toilet—you have. It takes a low-tech approach to life, placing emphasis on the character, not the contemporary components of a room, so it doesn't matter if you don't have the latest power shower or sleek mixer faucets. If you are completely revamping your bathing space, you can find old basins, bathtubs, faucets, toilet bowls and tanks at salvage yards. Many yards sell metal tubs freshly reenameled, but if you find one you love with chipped enamel, it's possible to get it recoated by a specialist, either in situ or before you install it. Salvage yards typically sell the classic roll-top bathtub, with handsome claw feet and painted underside; this is a great way to introduce color to the room. If you have the space, consider installing one in the center of the bathroom for the wow factor, and put in double sinks, too—handy for a large family.

THIS PAGE *This bathroom is big enough to accommodate a large French sofa, perfect for perching on while your bath runs or you paint your toenails. A glass-fronted cupboard, found in an antique store, was probably intended for life in a kitchen or living space, but is ideal in a bathroom, offering ample storage and room to display colorful bottles and washbags.*

OPPOSITE LEFT *A small old wooden chair, its frame painted pink to match the walls, is topped with towels and an enamel can, used to hold brushes.*

OPPOSITE RIGHT *A patterned towel can take a simple bathroom from plain to pretty in an instant. A beaded hanging basket set, suspended from the towel rod, stores bathing essentials close to the tub.*

THIS PAGE *Woven baskets are a great addition to any bathroom. They bring a welcome splash of bright color to an often neutral space and offer lots of room to hide your essentials. This lidded basket is from India, while the blue laundry basket is made of woven plastic, so it's waterproof, too—ideal in a bathing space.*

OPPOSITE *This lovely old drawer unit came from a thrift shop in England. It has lots of drawers for hiding away bathroom bits that don't lend themselves to display (cotton swabs, razors, toothpaste tubes) and handy hooks for hanging washbags from. On top, old perfume bottles and three floral pictures add another layer of decoration to this bathroom.*

Many bathrooms, particularly in city apartments, don't have a window. Even with one, the bathroom is still a space that requires good, versatile lighting. For nighttime ablutions, install wall lights around a mirror or above a sink and rely on a simple ceiling light for when you're bathing or mooching around. Install a dimmer switch so you can turn it down low for snoozy soaks and light a few candles for lots of atmosphere. Hang a mirror to help bounce light around. A large, plain mirror screwed to the wall behind a basin will also double as a backsplash. Freestanding lights are a no-no in a bathroom, and wall and ceiling lights should be steam- and moisture-resistant, so you will need to hit the mall, not the flea market, for those.

Don't forget storage. Bathrooms are home to all sorts of daily essentials—from toothpaste to razors and toilet paper—and, unlike the colorful mugs of a kitchen or the beautiful clothes of a bedroom, they are not particularly decorative. So get creative

with storage and tuck beauty products and basics away in wall-hung cabinets or a chest of drawers, dug up at a market and refreshed with a coat of paint. Use woven plastic baskets in rainbow colors (try ethnic shops) or large ceramic bowls, too. Remember to pick pieces in moisture-resistant materials such as painted wood, plastic, wicker, or glass. Soft woven baskets, invaluable in other rooms, can get moldy in a bathroom's steamy environment, and metal boxes and canisters can rust.

Once you have concealed the bottles of mouthwash and cans of shaving foam, you can have fun inventing ways to store and display your better-looking bathroom basics. Pile up multicolored towels on a shelf or bench. Put up peg rails or vintage hooks to hang body brushes and shower gels from. Add a folding patio chair or stool to perch on while the tub fills. Throw in a colorful mat, hang an ornate mirror, pictures to gaze at while you soak, even just a vase of flowers. A small white bowl or pretty tile can

ABOVE AND RIGHT *A simple rectangular basin teamed with cool, classic limestone on the walls and surfaces is a great starting point for any bathroom. Here, the mellow look has been revved up with colored plastic boxes and accessories and an ornate mirror.*

British Red Cross

First Aid Kit

ABOVE AND LEFT *The bathroom in this Thirties apartment has original paneled walls and a decorative leaded window. To complement, but not overpower, those features, the owner has added a simple contemporary basin. The plexiglass cross, hung from the ceiling, adds a splash of red, reflected in the cabinet.*

work well as a soap dish, old jugs and jars can house toothbrushes, and a simple white towel can get a bazaar-style update if you stitch on machine-washable colored trim.

Look for retro and vintage pieces that were designed for bathroom life, too. Lloyd Loom laundry baskets, old perfume bottles, shaving mirrors, medicine cabinets, and first-aid boxes all make regular appearances in thrift stores and flea markets. Enjoy mixing pieces from across the eras, whether they were intended for the bathroom or not, to create a space that's functional, but pleasing to all the senses.

THIS PAGE *Bazaar-style sleeping spaces often mix patterns—layering them on a bed means that no single design dominates the space, but all have a chance to be enjoyed. The red print of the Pakistani bedspread and the Indian wall hanging are balanced by crisp white bedlinen with blue embroidery. The pillows add some summer-of-love nostalgia.*

OPPOSITE LEFT *A big leather floor cushion in neutral white is teamed with hot pink and mellow gold cushions, colors that also show up in the rug, basket, and child's chair in this pretty bedroom.*

OPPOSITE RIGHT *Pile on the pattern on beds, but look for a theme to help them work together. Soft floral prints cohabit happily here.*

SLEEPING SPACES

While bazaar style is all about mixing objects, colors, and patterns, it is not about a design free-for-all. It's a look that loves visual variety, but not visual chaos, and nowhere is this more relevant than in the bedroom. Sleeping spaces need to be restful and calm. Strong colors or lively patterns should be tempered by neutral tones, and pockets of display should be balanced by unadorned space.

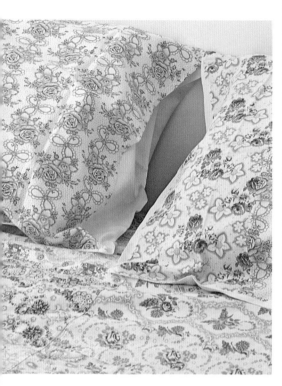

ABOVE *This traditional Dutch fabric has a small, detailed pattern that provides background color when viewed from a distance and lots of visual interest up close. Different examples of the fabric have been cut and stitched together to create a patchwork-effect duvet cover and pillowcases.*

RIGHT *This striking artwork dominates the room and dictates its colors. The white and wine shades of the picture are repeated in the bedlinen, pillows, and fluffy throw.*

LEFT *Inexpensive furry blankets from a local market warm up this bed in a Moroccan house. The rich red in the bedding is matched by a rosy red on the walls, creating a warm, enveloping atmosphere. Plain white pillowcases add some freshness and cool the crimson down.*

This means that if you cover your bed with decorative throws and pillows, it's a good idea to keep the walls pale and plain. If you hang patterned wallpaper or dramatic artwork, go for simple white bedlinen. If you group pretty pots and vases on a dressing table, store day-to-day bottles and beauty products out of sight. To keep the room relaxing, an eye for balance is essential.

Finding the visual interest in the objects that naturally belong to each room is a central theme of bazaar style. In the kitchen, china and flatware can take center stage. In a bedroom, clothes, shoes, and jewelry are the stars. They give the room its identity as a place to rest, potter, and dress, so it's good to display them. Hang a delicate blouse from a cupboard door or arrange

colorful handbags along a mantelpiece. Choose shelves that show off your favorite pieces combined with closed cupboards for the less interesting elements of your wardrobe (nobody needs their socks on display). Open shelves also make it easy to see everything—no more rummaging in the back of the closet. Combining beauty and practicality in this way is something bazaar style does well.

You may choose to keep your sleeping space just that—a place dedicated to sleep. In this case, a bed, bedside table, and a couple of lamps are all you need to create a tranquil room. Find a show-stopping bed at an antique shop or heap a mix of beautiful bedlinen from contemporary and vintage sources onto a simple

THIS PAGE *A simple mattress on the floor, spread with a beautiful bedspread and brightened up with colorful pillows, is all this Moroccan bedroom needs. Walls are kept clear and neutral, creating a strong sense of height and space. Pebbles gathered on the beach and hung on a string make a fittingly organic decoration for the entry.*

OPPOSITE LEFT *Positioning a bed against a chimney breast has one clear advantage: the recesses on each side can be used for storing bedtime books, magazines, and lighting. As with so many bazaar-style bedrooms, simple white bedding is the starting point for this bed, with interest added through a colorful throw.*

OPPOSITE RIGHT *Stools make perfect bedside tables since they are just the right height to be easily reached when in bed.*

frame to inject plenty of bazaar style, then keep the room clear. Store your make-up and beauty products in the bathroom and create a dressing area in a spare room, where you can hang clothes and keep shoes and other essentials such as a hairdryer. The message your bedroom sends will be clear—this is a space dedicated to sleep, rest, and sensuality; very separate from the rest of the house.

Most of us, with space at a premium, make our bedroom work a little harder. The bedroom is generally the place where we keep our clothes, where we sleep, dress, and read. While it has great practical purpose, it is also often an area used only in the morning and evening. However, if you choose the essential ingredients—the bed, lighting, and flooring—well, work in a modicum of display and plenty of sensual texture, you may be surprised by how much more you use it. Find space for a comfy armchair or chaise, and your room can become somewhere you go to read the paper, escape the TV, or just gaze out of the window.

The dominant feature of any sleeping space is the bed. We spend about a third of our lives in bed, so the mattress needs to be comfortable. Invest in the best-quality mattress you can afford, then recoup some pennies by picking up a secondhand frame. From old metal hospital beds to French carved wooden ones, there's a style to suit every wallet. Alternatively, buy a simple divan base and layer on floor-skimming sheets, blankets,

THIS PAGE *This cozy bedroom has lots of personality, thanks to the pattern-rich cushions and throw across the bed. Small square recesses cut into the wall (there is attic space behind) provide storage for books and a bedtime drink. The pigeon light is by Ed Carpenter.*

OPPOSITE LEFT *There is plenty of pattern in this bedroom, but it shares a loose theme—florals against a white background—to keep the look cohesive. The curtains are made from vintage fabric bought at a flea market, and the bedside table is from Morocco.*

OPPOSITE RIGHT *Patterned curtains liven up any bedroom. Teamed with white walls and simple bedding, they make a strong but pretty feature.*

and bedspreads to hide its plain appearance. For a bazaar look with a whiff of nostalgia, find faded eiderdowns and floral quilts, old linen sheets that are gloriously soft, crocheted blankets, and embroidered pillowcases at flea markets and vintage shops. They can all be dry-cleaned to refresh them, while cotton and linen sheets can simply be machine-washed. To bring a touch of Morocco or the Middle East to the room, choose strong, saturated colors and ethnic prints on cushions, flat woven rugs, and bedspreads. And forget matching sets. A motley collection of bedding looks great and is always ready—grab the first sheets, pillowcases, and blankets on the pile and just put them together.

When it comes to storage, the bazaar look favors the freestanding. Furniture that can move around, that is flexible and adaptable, is central to any bazaar-style room. Hunt for pieces with personality—an ornate French armoire, a tall chest of drawers with bun feet, a cavernous blanket box—or buy something cheap that can be modified. Remember, when you're looking for furniture, to concentrate on finding the shape you like, not the finish, as it can always be painted, papered, or treated to new knobs or handles. To give a plain armoire or cupboard a new look, cut out sections of its doors and replace with chicken wire, or remove the door and hang a patterned curtain instead.

ABOVE LEFT *Hanging a beautiful dress or colorful hats and bags from closet doors or a coat rail is an easy way to bring pattern and vibrancy to a sleeping space. It's flexible, too—just hang different clothes every day—and gives the room a strong identity as somewhere to dress and potter.*

ABOVE RIGHT *Shoes and handbags are designed to be decorative, and look great arranged on open shelves. It's also easy to find the pair you want—no rummaging in the back of the closet.*

In a sleeping space the lighting needs to be gentle, but you will also need some task lighting for bedtime reading or looking in the mirror, and one fairly strong light so you can see to dress on dark winter mornings. If you have a central pendant light, dress it flamboyantly in a glittering chandelier or big, decorative shade, and install a dimmer switch so you can control its brightness. Supplement it with table lamps on chests of drawers, a mantelpiece, or dressing table, so you can vary the mood. Gather bases in a selection of styles, then crown them with pretty patterned shades so they look as good switched off as on. You will certainly need a light by your bed. Wall lights that can be angled to

THIS PAGE *This bedroom has all the ingredients of a gently feminine space—twinkling chandelier, floral pillows, fresh flowers, pretty shades—but without looking fussy or girly. A bold throw from Pakistan, mismatched pillows, and the knocked-about feel of the chest of drawers give the room a lived-in air that's far from prissy.*

shine on your book are practical, but a low lamp on a bedside table will do just as well; after all, it only needs to be bright enough to illuminate the pages—you don't want glare.

There is room for some decoration and display in a sleeping space, but as we have discussed, balance is key. This is a place where too much visual interest can be detrimental, creating an over-stimulating environment that is hard to relax and sleep in. To avoid this, choose pieces that can multitask, performing a useful function while also adding a dash of bazaar style. Use an

old glass cake stand to pile your make-up on and save space on your dressing table at the same time. Find old suitcases or hatboxes that can hold shoes or bags. Look out for ottomans, wooden chests, or wicker blanket boxes that offer lots of storage space and, when scattered with cushions, a place to sit, too. Take care not to let the room or surfaces become cluttered, though. A bazaar-style sleeping space has just the right combination of your personal things with clear space, color, and neutrality to guarantee a good night's rest.

THIS PAGE AND OPPOSITE RIGHT
An embroidered quilt, clothes and necklaces hanging on show, and bright bedside tables picked up in Morocco—all give this space a relaxed personality. The owner, who collects vintage fabric, has customized the lampshades by stitching on small panels of patterned material.

OPPOSITE LEFT *Coat rails don't just belong in halls. In this ensuite bathroom, a rail holds shower caps and pretty bags.*

OUTDOOR LIVING

Gardens used to be just for those with green thumbs, but these days we're more likely to treat them as an extra room. They can perform numerous roles—a play area for kids, somewhere to entertain, or a tranquil place to relax —and by borrowing ideas from indoors, perhaps even the furniture, textiles, and cushions, too, you can make your outside space into an extension of your home.

ABOVE LEFT *This garden is given a blue theme, thanks to a grass-style umbrella and a painted shed. Simple wooden furniture gets lots of bazaar style with cushions and a tablecloth made from fabric remnants and beading, designed by the house's owner.*

ABOVE RIGHT *A Chinese parasol and French wrought-iron chairs and a table are the centerpiece of this small town garden. Built-in benches, bordering the garden, supplement the seating without cluttering the space. The fabric covering all the cushions is deliberately bright and contemporary, to give this courtyard a modern twist.*

There are many ways to bring some bazaar style to your outdoor space, be it a balcony, city courtyard, or rolling country patch. When it comes to planting, potted plants are ideal. Hundreds of plants, herbs, and small shrubs work well in pots rather than planted in a bed, and grown this way they are movable, too, so you can shift them around to create zones and generate visual variety. In a small city garden, which may be paved or decked entirely, they are the best way to introduce some natural color and texture, while in a larger patch they can soften the hard lines of patio borders and create pockets of interest.

Flea markets are great places to look for tubs, troughs, and containers. You will also spot plenty of vessels that can be

reinvented as plant pots. Old metal pails, tea caddies, baskets, wooden crates, ceramic sinks: anything that can hold soil can nurture a plant. If the material allows, pierce holes in the bottom for drainage, but before you get carried away and plant up an old tin bathtub, consider its weight, especially if you are putting pots on a balcony or roof terrace. Large vessels or those made from heavy stoneware can weigh a great deal. Is your space strong enough to support a full container? Could you move it if you wanted to? If not, you can buy wheeled caddies for heavy pots.

Seating is essential in even the smallest outdoor space, and it's worth considering building it in—a great way to create some structure in your outside room. Just build a low platform along

ABOVE LEFT *Standard wooden patio furniture can get a bazaar feel by being liberally covered with a bright throw from India and chunky cushions in striped fabric and pretty English florals by Cath Kidston. The parasol is also Indian.*

ABOVE RIGHT *A pile of pillows softens the built-in bench in this Moroccan roof terrace. The bold, almost retro fabrics are actually contemporary Moroccan designs, picked up in a local market. The surprise of finding them here, instead of the more predictable kilim fabric one usually sees in Moroccan homes, adds to their appeal.*

ABOVE LEFT *A shot of brilliant magenta makes a bold but pleasing contrast to this chair's leafy, natural surroundings.*

ABOVE RIGHT *Create a simple garden bench along one wall by laying planks across stacked-up breeze blocks, then pile on cushions for comfort. These are from Morocco.*

OPPOSITE *Design tricks that work indoors can do just as well outdoors. Hanging a mirror will make an enclosed garden seem bigger and brighter, while painting garden walls can influence the mood of the space. Introducing color with pillows and an Indian throw is an easy way to lift the feel of a outside space, too —no need for flowering plants.*

a fence or house wall and cover it with quilts, rugs, and cushions. You could also get some storage built in underneath so you can stash furniture away easily at night or in the winter. Supplement this with flexible seating and a table, too. Old deckchairs, wooden benches and tables, French café chairs and tables in wood or wrought iron, and wicker armchairs—all turn up in flea markets. Remember that, unless the furniture you find is weatherproof or made of hard-wearing wood such as teak, it will need to be stored under cover. You could choose pieces that will work indoors, too, or create some outside storage space—a brightly painted shed, perhaps—to keep them in good shape until spring comes.

Reclamation yards are good hunting grounds for patio furniture, too, and you may also find garden tools, interesting

ornaments, planters, and paving stones. Do check that the retailer makes sure that all items for sale have been legally sourced (see Source Directory for a list of reclamation yards and other salvage outlets). There has been a big trade in stolen outdoor furniture, statuary, and ornaments in recent years, so check the provenance before buying.

Color is at the heart of bazaar style, and in an outdoor space that need not come just from the planting. In a small city garden, paint fences or walls in rich Moroccan shades of turquoise, rose, and sand. Look for painted Lloyd Loom furniture or warm up plain wooden chairs with colorful cushions. If your garden is overlooked, draw the eye away from the surrounding buildings by laying bright floor cushions, colorful blankets, and simple rush mats on decking, lawn, or paving. Create cohesion by finding

color themes, too, just as you would indoors. Match foliage and flowers to a favorite picnic mat, zingy deckchair fabric, or a patterned hammock or awning.

Finally, you can use some of the bazaar-style tricks and techniques that work well indoors in your outdoor space, too. Hang a large mirror on a boundary or house wall to increase the sense of space and light in an enclosed garden. Drape baubles and glitter balls from trees to catch the sunlight and create some sparkle. Dot a table with favorite ornaments and pitchers filled with flowers. Then set the scene for romantic evening dining with plenty of candles. To prevent them from blowing out, pop them into votive holders or storm lanterns, metal lanterns or old jars. If biting insects are spoiling your supper, light citronella candles—their sharp, lemony smell will keep bugs at bay.

THIS PAGE *This outdoor pool is given a frivolous feel with pink-painted walls and seating. Woven plastic baskets, a bathroom staple, work brilliantly here, too—they are capacious, colorful, and water-resistant.*

OPPOSITE, ABOVE LEFT *Bazaar style believes in layering on pattern and color. The outside is no exception, so even if your garden is brimming with flowers there is room for a few more blooms on cushions.*

OPPOSITE, BELOW LEFT *Candles come into their own during twilight mealtimes. Pop them into storm lanterns, old bottles, or votive holders, to protect the flames from gusts.*

OPPOSITE, ABOVE AND BELOW RIGHT *Any material that can reflect the sunlight will add sparkle and visual texture to your outdoor space, whether that be colored glass tumblers or shiny metal balls hung from a branch.*

SOURCE DIRECTORY

A selection of thrift stores, secondhand shops, and flea markets ranging from thrifty to tony can be found in most cities and towns. Venture just a little way out of the city center with its chain stores and you'll find them. Check in local papers, too, or on community notice boards for listings of weekend tag or stoop sales, jumble sales, and street fairs.

You'll want to visit flea markets, antiques sales, and auctions. Some famous U.S. fairs are listed below. You can also check out www.fleamarket.com or http://goodridgeguides.com/fleamarketusa for a national directory of flea markets, swap meets, and trade days. When traveling, the local Chamber of Commerce can be an excellent source for information on rummage sales.

Selina Lake
Interior Stylist
+44 (0)7971 447785
www.selinalake.co.uk

FLEA MARKETS AND FAIRS

Brimfield Antique & Collectible Show
Route 20, Brimfield, MA 01010
413-245-3436
www.brimfieldshow.com
This celebrated flea market runs for a week in May, July, and September.

French Market Community Flea Market
1008 North Peters Street
New Orleans, LA 70116
504-522-2621
www.frenchmarket.org
Visit for locally made jewelry, clothing, and artefacts and the specialty shops that line the street.

Georgetown Flea Market
15th Street North between
Courthouse and North Veitch
Washington, D.C., 20037
202-775-FLEA
www.georgetownfleamarket.com
Featuring everything from bronzes to antique tools, Sundays from March through December.

The Manhattan Art and Antiques Center
1050 Second Avenue at
56th Street
New York, NY 10022
212-355-4400
www.the-maac.com
Large emporium selling an eclectic mix of period furniture, paintings, chandeliers, porcelain, and more.

Picc-a-dilly Flea Market
796 West 13th Street (Lane
County Fairgrounds), Eugene, OR
541-683-5589
www.planeteugene.com/
fleamarket.htm
Antiques, crafts, and collectibles, including fabrics, every Sunday, except in July and August.

Rose Bowl Flea Market
100 Rose Bowl Drive
Pasadena, CA
www.rgcshows.com/
RoseBowlFleaMarket
Everything from retro kitsch to fine antique furniture, on the second Sunday of each month.

RECLAMATION YARDS
AND SALVAGE

Architectural Accents
2711 Piedmont Road NE
Atlanta, GA 30305
404-266-8700
www.architecturalaccents.com
Antique light fixtures, door hardware, garden antiques, and other reclaimed items.

Architectural Antiques
1900 Linwood Avenue
Oklahoma City, OK 73109
405-232-0759
Architectural antiques, salvage, and curiosities.

Caravati's
104 East Second Street
Richmond, VA 23224
804-232-4175
www.caravatis.com
Materials and architectural details from old buildings.

Château Domingue
3615-B West Alabama Street
Houston, TX 77027
713-961-3444
www.chateaudomingue.com
Architectural elements, furnishings, and accessories.

Salvage One
1840 West Hubbard
Chicago, IL 60622
312-733-0098
www.salvageone.com
Architectural artefacts.

United House Wrecking
535 Hope Street
Stamford, CT 06906
203-348-5371
www.unitedhousewrecking.com
Reclaimed architectural fragments.

ANTIQUE, VINTAGE, AND
RETRO FURNITURE AND
ACCESSORIES

Bobbie King Antiques
667 Duling Avenue
Jackson, MS 39216
601-362-9803
Antique and contemporary collectibles and furnishing.

Bremermann Designs
3943 Magazine Street
New Orleans, LA 70015
504-891-7763
www.bremermanndesigns.com
French antiques and homewares.

Country Garden Antiques
147 Parkhouse Street
Dallas, TX 75207
214-741-9331
Cottage-style shabby chic antiques.

Design Within Reach
Call 800-944-2233 or visit
www.dwr.com to find a retail
outlet near you.
Design Within Reach gives you access to well-designed modernist furnishings traditionally found only in designers' showrooms.

Herman Miller
Call 616-654-3860 or visit the
website to find an outlet near you.
www.hermanmiller.com
Official U.S. importer of Artek furniture, also Charles and Ray Eames, Alvar Aalto, and other fine 20th-century furniture designers.

Newel Art Galleries
425 East 53rd Street
New York, NY 10022
212-758-1970
www.newel.com
A six-story building housing antiques from many periods and nations.

Retromodern.com
805 Peachtree Street, NE
Atlanta, GA 30308
404-724-0093
www.retromodern.com
Online retailer of reissues and current productions of modern Scandinavian designs by Fritz Hansen, iitala, Stelton, and more.

Richard B. Arkway
59 East 54th Street,
Suite 62
New York, NY 10022
212-751-8135
www.arkway.com
Antique maps, globes, atlases, rare books, and other curiosities.

Unica Home
7540 Dean Martin Drive,
Suite 501
Las Vegas, NV 89139
888-89-UNICA
www.unicahome.com
A wide range of mid-century modern furniture and accessories, both vintage and reproductions.

CONTEMPORARY AND REPRODUCTION FURNITURE AND ACCESSORIES

ABC Carpet & Home
Visit www.abchome.com for a retail outlet near you.
An eclectic collection of accessories for the home representing a winning diversity of periods and styles.

Anthropologie
Call 800-309-2500 to find a store near you or visit www.anthropologie.com.
Select mix of often vintage-inspired one-of-a-kind home accessories and decorative details.

Bombay
Call 800-956-1782 or visit www.bombaycompany.com to find a store near you.
Reproductions of classic, often British colonial-style home furnishings and accessories.

Charles P. Rogers
55 West 17th Street
New York, NY 10011
212-675-4400
www.charlesprogers.com
Brass, iron, and wood bed frames, from classic to contemporary.

Conran Shop
407 East 59th Street
New York, NY 10022
212-755-7249
www.conranusa.com
Well-designed contemporary furniture and accessories.

Pottery Barn
Call 888-779-5176 or visit www.potterybarn.com for a retail outlet near you.
Contemporary furniture and home accessories with a world beat.

Urban Outfitters
Call 800-282-2200 to find the retail outlet near you or visit www.urbanoutfitters.com.
Playful, affordable home details and furnishings that follow interior trends, including Moroccan chic and Paris flea market style.

West Elm
888-922-4119
www.westelm.com
Contemporary furniture and accessories featuring clean design and international flair.

Wunderley
128 Wilson Avenue
Greensburg, PA 15601
724-850-9616
www.wunderley.com
Moroccan and Middle Eastern mosaic and wood inlay furniture and accents.

LIGHTING

Antique Lighting Company
8214 Greenwood Avenue North
Seattle, WA 98103
800-224-7880
www.antiquelighting.com
Replicas of beautiful antique fixtures and custom lighting.

Continuum Antiques and Collectibles
7 Route 28
Orleans, MA 02653
508-255-8513
www.oldlamp.com
An antique lighting shop.

Eron Johnson Antiques
451 North Broadway
Denver, CO 80203
303-777-8700
www.eronjohnsonantiques.com
Antiques and curiosities, including table lamps, wall sconces, candelabra, chandeliers, and more.

The Moroccan Bazaar
972-599-2933
www.themoroccanbazaar.com
Moroccan chandeliers, lanterns, lamps, sconces, and other accessories, including room dividers and mirrors.

Revival Lighting
14 West Main Street
Spokane, WA 99201
888-747-4552
www.revivallighting.com
Large selection of restored vintage and antique lighting.

R 20th Century Design
82 Franklin Street
New York, NY 10013
212-343-7979
www.r20thcentury.com
Mid-century modern lamps and lighting fixtures.

WALLPAPER AND TEXTILES

Blink Décor
www.blinkdecor.com
Online retailer of wallpaper designs from antique glam to modern chic.

Blissliving Home
Call 866-95-BLISS for outlets.
www.blisslivinghome.com
Modern, globally inspired bedding, pillows, and other homewares.

Mombasa Net Canopies
399 North Great Southwest Parkway
Arlington, TX 76011
800-641-2345
www.mombasausa.net
Romantic bedhangings made from mosquito netting.

Osborne & Little
Call 203-359-1500 or visit www.osborneandlittle.com to locate a retailer near you.
Classic and contemporary fabrics and wallpapers for the Brit in you.

Pierre Deux
Call 888-743-7732 to find a retailer near you.
www.pierredeux.com
Fine French country wallpaper, fabric, upholstery, and antiques.

Secondhand Rose
138 Duane Street
New York, NY 10013
212-393-9002
www.secondhandrose.com
Huge collection of vintage wallpapers from Victorian to 1970s.

FLOORING

Flor
866-281-3567
www.flor.com
Check out Souk Chic rug tiles, composed of vibrant patchwork pieces of Turkish and Persian rugs.

Handcraft Tile
877-262-1140
www.handcrafttile.com
Antique and reproduction tiles.

Paris Ceramics
19 West Elm Street
Greenwich, CT 06830
203-862-9538 and branches
www.parisceramics.com
Limestone, terra cotta, antique stone, and hand-painted tiles.

Woven Accents
525 North La Cienega Boulevard
Los Angeles, CA 90048
310-652-6520
www.wovenonline.com
Antique and new handwoven rugs from India, Persia, and Morocco.

OUTDOOR LIVING

Archiped Classics
315 Cole Street
Dallas, TX 75207
214-748-7437
www.archipedclassics.com
Classic garden ornaments and furnishings, including cast stone urns, jardinieres, and pedestals.

Barbara Israel Garden Antiques
296 Mount Holly Road
Katonah, NY 10536
212-744-6281
www.bi-gardenantiques.com
Period garden ornaments and furniture from Europe, America, and Asia. By appointment only.

Elizabeth Street Garden and Gallery
209 Elizabeth Street
New York, NY 10012
212-941-4800
www.elizabethstreetgallery.com
Eclectic mix of antiques, including stone vessels and architectural ornaments for outdoors or in.

PICTURE CREDITS

Key: a=above, b=below, r=right, l=left, c=center.

All photography by Debi Treloar

Page 1 l the home of Joanne Cleasby, stallholder at Snooper's Paradise, Brighton; **1 cl** the home in Amsterdam of the stylist/artist Reineke Groters; **1 cr** www.juliaclancey.com; **1 r** private house in Amsterdam, owner Ank de la Plume; **2 row one: l** the London home of David and Jaz Bushell of Drapestar; **cl** Nikki Tibbles' London home, owner of Wild at Heart–Flowers and Interiors; **cr** Alan Higgs Architects; **r** www.juliaclancey.com; **2 row two: l & cl** the home of Netty Nauta in Amsterdam; **cr** www.juliaclancey.com; **r** Madeleine Rogers of Mibo; **2 row three: l & cr** the London home of Sam Robinson, co-owner of The Cross and Cross The Road; **cl** www.juliaclancey.com; **r** Nikki Tibbles' London home, owner of Wild at Heart–Flowers and Interiors; **2 row four: l** www.juliaclancey.com; **cl** the London home of Sam Robinson, co-owner of The Cross and Cross The Road; **cr** the home of Netty Nauta in Amsterdam; **r** the owners of Hope & Greenwood, Miss Hope and Mr Greenwood's home in London; **4–5 a** the home of Isobel Trenouth, her husband, and their four children; **5 c** www.juliaclancey.com; **5 b** the London home of Louise Scott-Smith of www.lovelylovely.co.uk; **12 row one: l & r** the home in Amsterdam of the stylist/artist Reineke Groters; **cl** the home of Isobel Trenouth, her husband, and their four children; **cr** the London home of Sam Robinson, co-owner of The Cross and Cross The Road; **12 row two: l** the London home of Sam Robinson, co-owner of The Cross and Cross The Road; **cl** private house in Amsterdam, owner Ank de la Plume; **cr** the home of Isobel Trenouth, her husband, and their four children; **r** the London home of Louise Scott-Smith of www.lovelylovely.co.uk; **12 row three: l** Alan Higgs Architects; **cl** the home of Isobel Trenouth, her husband, and their four children; **cr** the London home of Sam Robinson, co-owner of The Cross and Cross The Road; **r** Madeleine Rogers of Mibo; **12 row four: l** Nikki Tibbles' London home, owner of Wild at Heart–Flowers and Interiors; **cl** private house in Amsterdam, owner Ank de la Plume; **cr** the home in Amsterdam of the stylist/artist Reineke Groters; **r** Riad Chambres d'Amis in Marrakech (B&B), designed and owned by Ank de la Plume, decorated in co-production with Household Hardware and Rutger Jan de Lange; **14 & 15 b** the home of Netty Nauta in Amsterdam; **15 a** the home of Sarah O'Keefe, co-owner of The Cross in West London; **16 l** the home in Amsterdam of the stylist/artist Reineke Groters; **16 r & l** Nikki Tibbles' London home, owner of Wild at Heart–Flowers and Interiors; **17–18** www.juliaclancey.com; **19 a** the home of Joanne Cleasby, stallholder at Snooper's Paradise, Brighton; **19 bl** Alan Higgs Architects; **19 br** Nikki Tibbles' London home, owner of Wild at Heart–Flowers and Interiors; **20 l** the London home of Sam Robinson, co-owner of The Cross and Cross The Road; **20 r** the London home of Louise Scott-Smith of www.lovelylovely.co.uk; **21 l** the owners of Hope & Greenwood, Miss Hope and Mr Greenwood's home in London; **21 r** Nikki Tibbles' London home, owner of Wild at Heart–Flowers and Interiors; **22** the London home of Louise Scott-Smith of www.lovelylovely.co.uk; **23 l** the home of Netty Nauta in Amsterdam; **23 r** the London home of Louise Scott-Smith of www.lovelylovely.co.uk; **24 l** Nikki Tibbles' London home, owner of Wild at Heart–Flowers and Interiors; **24 r** the London home of Sam Robinson, co-owner of The Cross and Cross The Road; **25** Nikki Tibbles' London home, owner of Wild at Heart–Flowers and Interiors; **26 & 27 r** the home of Sarah O'Keefe, co-owner of The Cross in West London; **27 l** the home of Isobel Trenouth, her husband, and their four children; **28** the London home of Sam Robinson, co-owner of The Cross and Cross The Road; **29 l** private house in Amsterdam, owner Ank de la Plume; **29 r** Riad Yima, owned and designed by Hassan Hajjaj and managed by Abdelghafour Benbadryef, is available to rent; **30 l** the home in Amsterdam of the stylist/artist Reineke Groters; **30 r** the home of Sarah O'Keefe, co-owner of The Cross in West London; **31** the home of Netty Nauta in Amsterdam; **32** Nikki Tibbles' London home, owner of Wild at Heart–Flowers and Interiors; **33** Alan Higgs Architects; **34 l** the London home of Louise Scott-Smith of www.lovelylovely.co.uk; **34 r** Madeleine Rogers of Mibo; **35 l** the home of Joanne Cleasby, stallholder at Snooper's Paradise, Brighton; **35 r** Riad Chambres d'Amis in Marrakech (B&B), designed and owned by Ank de la Plume, decorated in co-production with Household Hardware and Rutger Jan de Lange; **36 a & bl** the home in Amsterdam of the stylist/artist Reineke Groters; **36 br** the home of Isobel Trenouth, her husband, and their four children; **37** the London home of Louise Scott-Smith of www.lovelylovely.co.uk; **38 l** private house in Amsterdam, owner Ank de la Plume; **38 r** Dar Beida and Dar Emma, available to rent—www.castlesinthesand.com, interior designers Emma Wilson and Graham Carter; **39** the home of Isobel Trenouth, her husband, and their four children; **40–41** the home in Amsterdam of the stylist/artist Reineke Groters; **42–43** the London home of David and Jaz Bushell of Drapestar; **44 l** private house in Amsterdam, owner Ank de la Plume; **44 r** Alan Higgs Architects; **45 al** Nikki Tibbles' London home, owner of Wild at Heart–Flowers and Interiors; **45 ar** the London home of David and Jaz Bushell of Drapestar; **45 bl** the London home of Sam Robinson, co-owner of The Cross and Cross The Road; **45 br** Riad Chambres d'Amis in Marrakech (B&B), designed and owned by Ank de la Plume, decorated in co-production with Household Hardware and Rutger Jan de Lange; **46 l** the home in Amsterdam of the stylist/artist Reineke Groters; **46 r** the home of Isobel Trenouth, her husband, and their four children; **47 l** Alan Higgs Architects; **47 r** Riad Chambres d'Amis in Marrakech (B&B), designed and owned by Ank de la Plume, decorated in co-production with Household Hardware and Rutger Jan de Lange; **48 l** the London home of Sam Robinson, co-owner of The Cross and Cross The Road; **48 r** www.juliaclancey.com; **49 l** Nikki Tibbles' London home, owner of Wild at Heart–Flowers and Interiors; **50** www.juliaclancey.com; **51** the home of Netty Nauta in Amsterdam; **52 l** private house in Amsterdam, owner Ank de la Plume; **52 r** the home of Netty Nauta in Amsterdam; **53** Alan Higgs Architects; **54 al** the home in Amsterdam of the stylist/artist Reineke Groters; **54 ar** Madeleine Rogers of Mibo; **54 bl** the owners of Hope & Greenwood, Miss Hope and Mr Greenwood's home in London; **54 br–56** www.juliaclancey.com; **57 l** Madeleine Rogers of Mibo; **57 r** the London home of Sam Robinson, co-owner of The Cross and Cross The Road; **58** the home in Amsterdam of the stylist/artist Reineke Groters; **59** www.juliaclancey.com; **60** the London home of Sam Robinson, co-owner of The Cross and Cross The Road; **61** www.juliaclancey.com; **62–63 l** the London home of Sam Robinson, co-owner of The Cross and Cross The Road; **63 r** Riad Chambres d'Amis in Marrakech (B&B), designed and owned by Ank de la Plume, decorated in co-production with Household Hardware and Rutger Jan de Lange; **64 l** the London home of Sam Robinson, co-owner of The Cross and Cross The Road; **64 r** www.juliaclancey.com; **65 l** the home of Joanne Cleasby, stallholder at Snooper's Paradise, Brighton; **65 r** Madeleine Rogers of Mibo; **66 l** the home of Joanne Cleasby, stallholder at Snooper's Paradise, Brighton; **66 l–r** Nikki Tibbles' London home, owner of Wild at Heart–Flowers and Interiors; **67** the owners of Hope & Greenwood, Miss Hope and Mr Greenwood's home in London; **68** Riad Chambres d'Amis in Marrakech (B&B), designed and owned by Ank de la Plume, decorated in co-production with Household Hardware and Rutger Jan de Lange; **69 al** the home of Joanne Cleasby, stallholder at Snooper's Paradise, Brighton; **69 ar** private house in Amsterdam, owner Ank de la Plume; **69 bl** the London home of Louise Scott-Smith of www.lovelylovely.co.uk; **69 br** the home in Amsterdam of the stylist/artist Reineke Groters; **70 row one: l** the London home of Sam Robinson, co-owner of The Cross and Cross The Road; **cl** the home of Sarah O'Keefe, co-owner of The Cross in West London; **cr & r** the London home of Louise Scott-Smith of www.lovelylovely.co.uk; **70 row two: l & cr** the home of Sarah O'Keefe, co-owner of The Cross in West London; **cl** Dar Beida and Dar Emma, available to rent—www.castlesinthesand.com, interior designers Emma Wilson and Graham Carter; **r** the London home of Sam Robinson, co-owner of The Cross and Cross The Road; **70 row three: l** Riad Chambres d'Amis in Marrakech (B&B), designed and owned by Ank de la Plume, decorated in co-production with Household Hardware and Rutger Jan de Lange; **cl** the London home of Sam Robinson, co-owner of The Cross and Cross The Road; **cr** the owners of Hope & Greenwood, Miss Hope and Mr Greenwood's home in London; **r** the home of Isobel Trenouth, her husband, and their four children; **70 row four: l & r** the home in Amsterdam of the stylist/artist Reineke Groters; **cl** the London home of Louise Scott-Smith of www.lovelylovely.co.uk; **cr** the home of Sarah O'Keefe, co-owner of The Cross in West London; **72** the London home of Sam Robinson, co-owner of The Cross and Cross The Road; **73** Dar Beida and Dar Emma, available to rent—www.castlesinthesand.com, interior designers Emma Wilson and Graham Carter; **74–75** private house in Amsterdam, owner Ank de la Plume; **76 l** the owners of Hope & Greenwood, Miss Hope and Mr Greenwood's home in London; **77 r** the home of Isobel Trenouth, her husband, and their four children; **77 l** www.juliaclancey.com; **77 r** the London home of Louise Scott-Smith of www.lovelylovely.co.uk; **78–79** Alan Higgs Architects; **80** Dar Beida and Dar Emma, available to rent—www.castlesinthesand.com, interior designers Emma Wilson and Graham Carter; **81** the home of Joanne Cleasby, stallholder at Snooper's Paradise, Brighton; **82–83** the home of Sarah O'Keefe, co-owner of The Cross in West London; **84–85** Riad Chambres d'Amis in Marrakech (B&B), designed and owned by Ank de la Plume, decorated in co-production with Household Hardware and Rutger Jan de Lange; **86** the home in Amsterdam of the stylist/artist Reineke Groters; **88–89** the London home of Sam Robinson, co-owner of The Cross and Cross The Road; **90–91** the home of Sarah

O'Keefe, co-owner of The Cross in West London; **92–93** private house in Amsterdam, owner Ank de la Plume; **94–95 l** the home of Joanne Cleasby, stallholder at Snooper's Paradise, Brighton; **95 r** Nikki Tibbles' London home, owner of Wild at Heart–Flowers and Interiors; **96–97** the home of Isobel Trenouth, her husband, and their four children; **98–99** Alan Higgs Architects; **100–101** Riad Chambres d'Amis in Marrakech (B&B), designed and owned by Ank de la Plume, decorated in co-production with Household Hardware and Rutger Jan de Lange; **102** Nikki Tibbles' London home, owner of Wild at Heart–Flowers and Interiors; **103 l** Riad Chambres d'Amis in Marrakech (B&B), designed and owned by Ank de la Plume, decorated in co-production with Household Hardware and Rutger Jan de Lange; **103 r** the home in Amsterdam of the stylist/artist Reineke Groters; **104 al** Nikki Tibbles' London home, owner of Wild at Heart–Flowers and Interiors; **104 ar** Nikki Tibbles' London home, owner of Wild at Heart–Flowers and Interiors; **104 bl** the owners of Hope & Greenwood, Miss Hope and Mr Greenwood's home in London; **104 br** the home of Isobel Trenouth, her husband, and their four children; **105** Riad Chambres d'Amis in Marrakech (B&B), designed and owned by Ank de la Plume, decorated in co-production with Household Hardware and Rutger Jan de Lange; **106 l** the home of Netty Nauta in Amsterdam; **106 r–107** the home in Amsterdam of the stylist/artist Reineke Groters; **108** private house in Amsterdam, owner Ank de la Plume; **109 l** the owners of Hope & Greenwood, Miss Hope and Mr Greenwood's home in London; **109 r** Madeleine Rogers of Mibo; **110** the home of Sarah O'Keefe, co-owner of The Cross in West London; **111** the home of Isobel Trenouth, her husband, and their four children; **112 l** the London home of Sam Robinson, co-owner of The Cross and Cross The Road; **112 r** the London home of Louise Scott-Smith of www.lovelylovely.co.uk; **113** the home of Sarah O'Keefe, co-owner of The Cross in West London; **114** the London home of Sam Robinson, co-owner of The Cross and Cross The Road; **115–116** private house in Amsterdam, owner Ank de la Plume; **117** the home of Joanne Cleasby, stallholder at Snooper's Paradise, Brighton; **118** the home of Sarah O'Keefe, co-owner of The Cross in West London; **119** the London home of Sam Robinson, co-owner of The Cross and Cross The Road; **120 l** private house in Amsterdam, owner Ank de la Plume; **120 r** the London home of David and Jaz Bushell of Drapestar; **121** Riad Yima, owned and designed by Hassan Hajjaj and managed by Abdelghafour Benbadryef, is available to rent; **122** Dar Beida and Dar Emma, available to rent—www.castlesinthesand.com, interior designers Emma Wilson and Graham Carter; **123 l** Riad Chambres d'Amis in Marrakech (B&B), designed and owned by Ank de la Plume, decorated in co-production with Household Hardware and Rutger Jan de Lange; **123 r** private house in Amsterdam, owner Ank de la Plume; **124** the London home of Louise Scott-Smith of www.lovelylovely.co.uk; **125–126 l** the home of Isobel Trenouth, her husband, and their four children; **126 r** the home of Netty Nauta in Amsterdam; **127** the London home of Sam Robinson, co-owner of The Cross and Cross The Road; **128–129** the home of Isobel Trenouth, her husband, and their four children; **130–131** Alan Higgs Architects; **132 l** the home of Isobel Trenouth, her husband, and their four children; **132 r & 133 l** the London home of Sam Robinson, co-owner of The Cross and Cross The Road; **133 r** Dar Beida and Dar Emma, available to rent—www.castlesinthesand.com, interior designers Emma Wilson and Graham Carter; **134 l** Alan Higgs Architects; **134 r–135** the home of Sarah O'Keefe, co-owner of The Cross in West London; **136 al** the home of Isobel Trenouth, her husband, and their four children; **136 ar** the London home of Sam Robinson, co-owner of The Cross and Cross The Road; **136 b–137** Alan Higgs Architects; **144 cl** the home in Amsterdam of the stylist/artist Reineke Groters; **144 cr** the London home of Louise Scott-Smith of www.lovelylovely.co.uk; **144 r** www.juliaclancey.com.

ARTISTS, DESIGNERS, AND RETAILERS WHOSE WORK IS FEATURED IN THIS BOOK

www.castlesinthesand.com
+44 (0)776 852190 (UK mobile)
+212 (0)679 65386 (Moroccan mobile)
For commissions, email
emma@castlesinthesand.com
38 right; 70 row two center left; 73; 122; 133 right.

www.chambresdamis.com
12 row four right; 35 right; 45 below right; 47 right; 63 right; 68; 70 row three left; 84–85; 100–101; 103 left; 105; 106 right–107; 123 left.

Joanne Cleasby at Snooper's Paradise
7–8 Kensington Gardens
Brighton BN1 4AL
+44 (0)1273 602558
1 left; 19 above; 35 left; 65 left; 66 left; 69 above left; 81; 94–95 left; 117.

www.drapestar.com
2 row one left; 42–43; 45 above right; 120 right.

Reineke Groters, stylist and artist
reineke.groters@zonnet.nl
1 center left; 12 row one left & right; 12 row four center right; 16 left; 29 left; 30 left; 36 above & below left; 40–41; 46 left; 54 above left; 58; 69 below right; 70 row four left & right; 86; 103 right.

Haberfield Hall
Haberfield Hall is available for hire as a photographic location for both still and moving film. Please contact

Helene Field at Shootspaces.
+44 (0)20 7912 9989
+44 (0)7880 636473
enquiries@shootspaces.com
www.shootspaces.com
4; 5 above; 12 row one center left; 12 row two center right; 12 row three center left; 27 left; 36 below right; 39; 46 right; 70 row three right; 77 right; 96–97; 104 below right; 111; 125–126 left; 128–129; 132 left; 136 above left.

Alan Higgs Architects Limited
173 Seymour Place
London W1H 4PW
+44 (0)20 7723 0075
fax +44 (0)20 7724 4290
mail@alanhiggsarchitects.com
www.alanhiggsarchitects.com
Team: Alan Higgs, David Weston-Thomas, Richard Nicholls
Sliding fabric panels in drawing room and living room by Ketcher and Moore; lighting design in drawing room by Light IQ.
2 row one center right; 12 row three left; 19 below left; 33; 44 right; 47 left; 53; 78–79; 98–99; 130–131; 134 left; 136 below–137.

Hope & Greenwood
Purveyors of Splendid Confectionery.
www.hopeandgreenwood.co.uk
2 row four right; 21 left; 54 below left; 67; 70 row three center right; 76 left; 104 below left; 109 left.

www.householdware.nl
1 right; 12 row two center left; 12 row four center left; 29 left; 38 left; 44 left; 52 left; 69 above right; 74–75; 92–93; 108; 115; 116; 120 left; 123 right.

www.juliaclancey.com
1 center right; 2 row one right; 2 row two center right; 2 row three center left; 2 row four left; 5 center; 17-18; 48 right; 50; 54 below right–56; 59; 61; 64 right; 77 left.

Lovelylovely
+44 (0)20 7482 6365
info@lovelylovely.co.uk
www.lovelylovely.co.uk
5 below; 12 row two right; 20 right; 22 & 23 right; 34 left; 37; 69 below left; 70 row one center right & right; 70 row four center left; 77 right; 112 right; 124.

Mibo
tel and fax +44 (0)8700 119620
info@mibo.co.uk
www.mibo.co.uk
2 row two right; 12 row three right; 34 right; 54 above right; 57 left; 65 right; 109 right.

Riad Yima
52 Derb Aarjane—Rahba Lkdima
40 000 Marrakech—Medina
+212 (0)24 39 19 87
and
LaRache Boutique
30–32 Calvert Avenue
London E2 7JP
+44 (0)20 7729 7349
hassanhajjaj@gmail.com

All the artizanas: Riaka and Saida (Morocco), Ekram (London)
29 right; 121.

Snooper's Paradise
7–8 Kensington Gardens
Brighton BN1 4AL
+44 (0)1273 602558
nic@internetdropshop.co.uk
6–11.

The Cross and Cross The Road
141 Portland Road
London W11 4LR
+44 (0)20 7727 6760
fax +44 (0)20 7727 6745
2 row three left & center right; 2 row four center left; 12 center right; 12 row two left; 12 row three center right; 20 left; 24 right; 26–27 right; 28; 30 right; 45 below left; 48 left; 57 right; 60; 62–63 left; 64 left; 70 row one left & center left; 70 row two left, right & center right; 70 row three center left; 70 row four center right; 72; 82–83; 88–89; 90–91; 112 left; 114; 118; 119; 127; 132 right & 133 left; 134 right–135; 136 above right.

The Turquoise Island
222 Westbourne Grove
London W11 2RJ
+44 (0)20 7727 3095
fax +44 (0)20 7792 8302
www.wildatheart.com
2 row one center left; 2 row three right; 12 row four left; 16 right; 19 below right; 21 right; 24 left; 25; 32; 45 above left; 49 left; 66 right; 95 right; 102; 104 above right.

INDEX

Figures in *italics* refer to the illustrations and captions.

ACKNOWLEDGMENTS

I would like to thank Alison Starling for realizing my *Bazaar Style* book idea and for giving me such an exciting opportunity. A massive thank you to Debi Treloar for all her beautiful photography, friendship, and humor, for being such great company in Brighton, Bristol, Amsterdam, and especially Morocco (and for the Caipirinha introduction!). Many thanks to Joanna Simmons for her witty and interesting words. A massive thank you to all at Ryland Peters & Small for their hard work and dedication to this project, including Jess Walton, Amy Trombat, Clare Double, Gemma John, and Leslie Harrington. I would like to personally thank all the generous people who gracefully welcomed us into their beautifully Bazaar homes.

On a personal note I would like to thank all my friends who have wished me luck and my lovely family for all their support and encouragement. Thank you, Mum, Dad, Aimee, and My Dave.

Selina Lake

Joanna Simmons' thanks go out to Alison Starling, for giving her the opportunity to write this book, to editor Clare Double for her diligence and good-naturedness, to Selina Lake for dreaming up the idea and making it come to life, and to Steve, for his patient support.